Martin Hanna and

Questions and Answers About

Women's Ordination

Pacific Press®
Publishing Association

Nampa, Idaho | Oshawa, Ontario, Canada
www.pacificpress.com

Cover design by Kristin Hansen-Mellish
Cover design resources from iStockphoto.com
Inside design by Carol Loree

Copyright © 2014 by Pacific Press® Publishing Association
Printed in the United States of America
All Rights Reserved

Unless otherwise noted, scriptures are taken from the New King James Version®. Copyright © 1982 by Thomas Nelson, Inc. Used by permission. All rights reserved.

Scripture quotations marked KJV are from the King James Version of the Bible.

Scriptures quoted from NASB are from *The New American Standard Bible*®, copyright © 1960, 1962, 1963, 1968, 1971, 1972, 1973, 1975, 1977, 1995 by The Lockman Foundation. Used by permission.

Scripture quotations marked NIV are from the HOLY BIBLE, NEW INTERNATIONAL VERSION®. Copyright © 1973, 1978, 1984 by International Bible Society. Used by permission of Zondervan Publishing House. All rights reserved.

Scripture quotations marked NLT are from the Holy Bible. New Living Translation, copyright © 1996, 2004, 2007, 2013 by Tyndale House Foundation. Used by permission of Tyndale House Publishers Inc., Carol Stream, Illinois 60188. All rights reserved.

The authors assume full responsibility for the accuracy of all facts and quotations as cited in this book.

You can obtain additional copies of this book by calling toll-free 1-800-765-6955 or by visiting http://www.adventistbookcenter.com.

ISBN 13: 978-0-8163-5726-0
ISBN 10: 0-8163-5726-9

September 2014

Contents

Acknowledgments	5
Preface	7
Introduction	11

Section I: Getting Started
The Big Picture	15
Hermeneutics: Principles to Guide Bible Study	20

Section II: The Old Testament
Creation	29
Sin and Salvation	35
Precedents	38

Section III: The New Testament
Creation	43
Sin and Salvation	46
Precedents	50
Headship	56
Pastors, Elders, and Deacons	60
Teaching Authority	66
Silent Women	68

Section IV: The Seventh-day Adventist Church
Ellen White	73
Seventh-day Adventist History	88
Current Discussion	96
The Way Forward	98

Works Cited	109
Appendix A	113
Appendix B	125
Online Resources for Further Study	159

Acknowledgments

Some cultures teach that it takes a village to raise a child, meaning that if a loving extended community of family and friends provides support to the parents, the child will be stronger for it. That concept is certainly true of *Questions and Answers About Women's Ordination.* Many students of the Bible worked prayerfully together to provide the answers to questions about the ordination of women found in this book.

We are especially grateful to Ángel Rodríguez, Denis Fortin, Dick Davidson, Carl Cosaert, Teresa Reeve, and Ron du Preez, for their work on several of the more contested answers. We are also indebted to Gordon Bietz and the North American Division Theology of Ordination Study Committee majority report. Other contributors we wish to thank include Nathan Brown, John Brunt, Darius Jankiewicz, Paul Petersen, Daniel Stojanovic, Tara VinCross, and Jim Wibberding. Colleagues in ministry, administration, and teaching helped us choose and prioritize the questions, using an interactive template developed by Julie Alvarez.

Many thanks to the Seventh-day Adventist Theological Seminary at Andrews University and to Gerry Chudleigh for granting permission to use their material in our appendices.

Laura Wibberding served ably as our consultant, providing excellent editing, writing, and organizing support. We also very much appreciate our typist, Joy Sorensen, and our external editor, Carol Loree.

Our deepest gratitude goes to our Savior, Jesus Christ, and to the Holy Spirit, upon whom we depended every step of this journey.

> Not unto us, O Lord, not unto us,
> But to Your name give glory,
> Because of Your mercy,
> Because of Your truth (Psalm 115:1, NKJV).

Preface

During the years that I worked as an associate director of the Ellen G. White Estate, I preached in 61 countries, in all 13 divisions of the Seventh-day Adventist world church. What a privilege to witness the unity of God's people amidst the diversity of culture, race, gender, and age!

You can imagine, then, how my heart ached to see my brothers and sisters in our community of faith so deeply divided—sometimes even to the point of acrimony—during our years of serving together on the Theology of Ordination Study Committee. How was it possible that "coldness, variance, strife" could replace the "sacred union with Christ" that unites us in the "bonds of Christian fellowship" (Ellen G. White, *Our Father Cares*, p. 124)? Some with whom I had previously partnered in mission and efforts to preserve historic Adventist positions now seemed certain that I had apostatized. I wanted to cry out: "Most of the people, myself included, who support gender-inclusive ministry also hold a high view of Scripture! We affirm the authority of the Word of God, the sacredness of the family, and the centrality of missions.[1] We believe strongly in a literal Creation week, a pre-Advent judgment, the inspiration of Ellen White, biblically defined marriage, and sexual activity confined to a married man and woman. We support and participate in the proclamation of Revelation's three angels. Lay down your fears!"

It was while praying and fasting about this spiritual crisis in our church that an administrator invited me to begin collecting biblical, historical, and inspiration-based evidence that would promote the character of our inclusive God.[2] I invited Dr. Martin Hanna, truly a Christlike, noncombative scholar, to join me in this quest for answers

Questions and Answers About Women's Ordination

to questions regarding the ordination of women and to promote a way forward that could unite the Advent movement in the urgent proclamation of the three angels' messages.

We were affirmed in our research by the Bible's own statements: "Search the Scriptures" (John 5:49, NKJV). "They ... searched the Scriptures daily, whether those things were so" (Acts 17:11, KJV). "Be ready always to give an answer" (1 Pet. 3:15, NKJV).

We found extraordinarily relevant statements in Ellen White's writings concerning our investigation, such as: "Whenever the people of God are growing in grace, they will be constantly obtaining a clearer understanding of His word. They will discern new light and beauty in its sacred truths.... But as spiritual life declines, it has ever been the tendency to cease to advance in the knowledge of the truth. Men rest satisfied with the light already received from God's word, and discourage any further investigation of the Scriptures. They become conservative, and seek to avoid discussion" (*Gospel Workers*, pp. 297-298). "Study the Scriptures for further light on this point [women in ministry]. Women were among Christ's devoted followers in the days of His ministry, and Paul makes mention of certain women who were helpers together with him in the gospel" (*Letter 142*, 1909, pp. 4-6; *Manuscript Releases*, Vol. 12, p. 167).

It was this Ellen White citation, however, that I found particularly intriguing: "In every age there is a new development of truth, a message of God to the people of that generation" (*Christ's Object Lessons*, p. 127).

What new development of truth could God be sending to our generation, to those of us living in a time of chaos, moral decay, and catastrophe?[3]

Could this "new light" be God now calling His people to break down every vestige of hierarchy and restore the Edenic plan of male-female relationships? Could we now seek restoration of the image of God, not just between people groups and ethnicities, but in ministry?

Could this "new light" include recognizing that God has never been

Preface

a respecter of persons in regard to whom He calls to ministry, but that whomever He calls is His ideal and not His last choice? Could this "new light" include a vindication of the character of God who makes no distinction between male and female when He anoints someone for service and leadership?

For Adventist Christians, the great hope, the good news, is the redemption theme, the restoration in humanity of the image of God. Since God's original creation included equality between the sexes, we could extrapolate from that pattern that it is His will that equal opportunities for ministry be presented in our present culture. We should then press on toward that ideal as part of our reception of the gospel.

This divisive issue has hindered our witness far too long! As a united people, we will become together that "army with banners" (Song 6:10) that proclaims the message of the righteousness of Christ, through the agency of the Holy Spirit in Latter Rain power. God Himself will take great delight in using whomever He wishes for whatever task to which He calls!

It is, then, in the spirit of forbearance, humility, and love for our church and in the honor of God's character that we offer this book.

Cindy Tutsch

---

1. Those who are in favor of women's ordination fully concur with, support, appropriate, and employ the 1986 Methods of Bible Study document voted by the Autumn Council.

2. Ellen White wrote that "the last message of mercy to be given to the world, is a revelation of [God's] character of love" (*Christ's Object Lessons*, p. 415).

3. Ellen White wrote: "We need now to begin over again. Reforms must be entered into with heart and soul and will. Errors may be hoary with age; but age does not make error truth, nor truth error" (*Testimonies for the Church*, Vol. 6, p. 142).

Introduction

From the time of the Millerite movement, Adventists have supported the involvement of women in evangelism and church ministry. There have never been large numbers of women in ministry, but there have always been some. During the first two decades after the Seventh-day Adventist Church was organized, the *Review and Herald* denominational journal periodically printed articles defending women in ministry or as public speakers in religious events with the argument that the gifts of the Spirit are all gender-inclusive. Ellen White also encouraged women to be active in any kind of ministry to win souls for Christ.

From the early years of our movement, women were involved in evangelism and many other facets of ministry, serving as conference secretaries, treasurers, departmental leaders, and even in management of churches. Women have served as associate pastors and have been admitted to our seminaries and schools of religion for preparation for pastoral ministry. Women have been encouraged to serve and be active in church ministry. Currently in many parts of the world, women serve as pastors of local congregations and as leaders of various ministries at all levels of the church.

Women began to receive a license to serve as Bible workers in 1868. Since then women have received a license or credential for their service in a variety of ministries. Through the years our understanding of the type of ministry for which we give a license or credential has changed for both men and women involved in church work.

Today, the Seventh-day Adventist world church is engaging in vigorous debate on the propriety of ordaining women called to gospel ministry. There are God-fearing Adventist scholars and laity on both

Questions and Answers About Women's Ordination

sides who believe they have found biblical support for their views. Thus, rigid all-or-none legislation on this topic has potential for splitting the church. There are some on both sides who regard their positions as so important that they are willing to risk such a split over this issue.

Splitting the church, however, does not portray the attitude of our Jesus—redemptive, unifying, Shepherd of all His people. Could it be that God has a new path? This path does not require a "yes" for women's ordination to be mandated in all places; and it does not require a "no" to the practice of women's ordination in some places.

This book sets forth that alternative path, providing biblical support for the ordination of women in areas of the world where this would enhance the mission and work of the church. We need not fear this alternative merely because it seems new. God's promise to ancient Israel may also be His promise to us: "I will lead blind Israel down a new path, guiding them along an unfamiliar way. I will brighten the darkness before them and smooth out the road ahead of them" (Isa. 42:16, NLT).

This new path allows for the church to remain united on the biblical truth summarized in our doctrines and united in our mission while allowing for diversity on the issue of the ordination of women. Were such unity in diversity on administrative matters to become policy, and the Spirit allowed to choose the gifts through which the three angels' messages will be proclaimed, how soon would the whole earth be lighted with the glory of God (see Rev. 18:1)!

As we contemplate the way forward, many questions have been asked, and answers to these questions have been proposed. Many of these questions and answers based on the inspired Word of God are presented in this book. It is our hope that this will be helpful to all who participate in prayerful and careful consideration of how God is leading His people with regard to the ordination of women for pastoral ministry.

Section I: Getting Started

The Big Picture

*"As God has distributed . . . so I ordain
in all the churches" (1 Cor. 7:17).*[1]

1. Does the call to ministry come from God or from human beings?

   Many examples from the Bible demonstrate that God calls people (Hos. 11:1) to His own service. He gives individual, often dramatic calls to His prophets (1 Sam. 3:4; Isa. 6:1-10; 49:1; Jer. 1:4-5). The Levites, although they were priests by birth, were chosen as a tribe for this service by God. The judges (Judg. 3:9), and even kings and dynasties (such as David's line), were specifically chosen by God for their work (2 Kings 9:6; 2 Chron. 22:7). In the New Testament, Jesus personally appointed His disciples (Mark 1:20), and intervened to call the apostle Paul to His service (Acts 13:1-2; 26:13-19). Persons for whom there is no recorded calling event, such as Timothy, are said to be called by God (1 Tim. 6:11-12).

2. What is the role of the church in the calling process initiated by God?

   The role of the church is to recognize and support God's call. In Acts 6, at the choosing of those who would do the work of deacons, the apostles recognized the working of the Spirit in those who were selected by the church and set them aside by the laying on of hands. When Jesus called Paul from being a persecutor of Christians to being a servant of the gospel, He personally intercepted him on the road to Damascus. In conjunction with this initiative, Jesus asked Ananias in Damascus to visit Paul and give him his new mission (Acts 9:1-19). In Antioch, "As they ministered to the Lord and fasted, the Holy Spirit said, 'Now separate to Me Barnabas and Saul for the work to which I have called them.' Then, having fasted and prayed, and laid hands on them, they sent them away" (13:2-3). In each of these cases we see God and the church working hand in hand, with God calling someone to ministry and the church affirming that call.

3. What is the purpose of church organization, including ordination?

Questions and Answers About Women's Ordination

As a part of church organization, the purpose of ordination is always to better serve the mission of the gospel. In Acts 6, individuals are chosen to do the work of deacons because there is too much work for the apostles to do, and they must specialize and delegate some tasks to other leaders. As the apostles preached and traveled, local leaders were appointed in the churches. By the end of the New Testament, the church had apostles and many other ministries regarded as gifts to the church from God (Eph. 4:7-12; Rom. 12:6-8; 1 Cor. 12:4-11). Appointing people to these responsibilities distributed authority to local settings and allowed the church to spread the gospel more effectively.

4. How is ordination as practiced today related to the biblical terminology associated with the call to ministry?

Although the word *ordination* does not appear in the Bible, the concept has been linked with biblical terms such as: "laying on of hands" (1 Tim. 4:14; 2 Tim. 1:6; Heb. 6:2), "set in order," "ordain/appoint" (Titus 1:5 KJV/NKJV). The Bible refers to the appointing or setting aside of someone for a particular purpose. First, God appoints someone; and then the church recognizes that appointment. The church can only ordain what God has already distributed in the church (1 Cor. 7:17). For example, Paul was already recognized as an apostle and teacher by the church when the Holy Spirit instructed them to set him aside for a specific task (Acts 13:1-3).

In the Seventh-day Adventist Church, ordination is more specific and denotes a certain level of denominational authority. This more specific use is for organizational purposes rather than theological ones; the designation of ordained ministers is meant to make the church more efficient in spreading the gospel.

5. Is there a difference between ordinations done in the Old Testament and those in the New Testament?

There are similarities and differences. There is similarity in that in both testaments, God calls and His people recognize and affirm that call. An important example of a difference is that in the New Testament, there is a change in the law with regard to the ordination of priests. "For the priesthood being changed, of necessity

Section I: Getting Started

there is also a change of the law" (Heb. 7:12).

6. Does God set/appoint/ordain those who exercise spiritual gifts in the church?

   Yes. The Greek words often translated "ordain" in the New Testament carry the idea of to "set" or "appoint." First Corinthians 12:28 tells us that "God has appointed these in the church: first apostles, second prophets, third teachers, after that miracles, then gifts of healings, helps, administrations, varieties of tongues."

7. Does God set/appoint/ordain women in the church to exercise spiritual gifts?

   God has set or appointed or ordained prophets in the church (1 Cor. 12:28), including female prophets. Note the references to "Miriam the prophetess" (Ex. 15:20), "Deborah, a prophetess" (Judg. 4:4), "Huldah the prophetess" (2 Kings 22:14), and "Anna, a prophetess" (Luke 2:36). Clearly, women have been ordained by God for the prophetic ministry in the church.

8. Does God set/appoint/ordain women to leadership roles other than prophet?

   Yes, many women serve God's people in leadership roles in the Bible. In the Old Testament, "Deborah, a prophetess … was judging" (Judg. 4:4). In the New Testament, many women served the early church as Paul's co-workers and had some leadership roles. Among them are Priscilla (Rom. 16:3), Mary (16:6), Tryphaena, Tryphosa and Persis (16:12), Euodia and Syntyche (Phil. 4:2).

9. Should the church ordain women in harmony with God's ordination of women?

   Yes. While the ordination of female pastors is not prescribed or prohibited, there are biblical principles that illuminate this issue. Jesus taught us to pray: "Your will be done on earth as it is in heaven" (Matt. 6:10). Also: "Whatever you bind on earth will be bound in heaven and whatever you loose on earth will be loosed in heaven" (16:19; 18:18). Paul writes: "As God has distributed … so I ordain in all the churches" (1 Cor. 7:17).

Questions and Answers About Women's Ordination

10. Should we regard ordination as important or necessary to ministry, or would we be better off to stop ordaining anyone?

    Ordination does not function in a magic sense, infusing into the minister some special power. At the same time, dedication for service, being officially shown by the corporate church—the community of believers—is personally inspiring. Ordination also implies that the organized church has spoken and appointed some people for certain functions. Without actions such as ordination, ecclesiastical order would be at risk. It would, however, be wrong to say that ordination is "just an appointment by the church." Such expression downgrades the value of the church and the reality of God's leading in the church.

11. What values should the church prioritize when making decisions about policies of ordination today?

    The church must first be biblical by acknowledging that God chooses whom He wants to do His work, and our role is simply to recognize that calling when we see it at work (Acts 13:1-3). This means using discernment to recognize the leading and the fruits of the Spirit in a candidate (6:3). Secondly, the church must keep the original purpose of church organization, including ordination, which is to be more effective at spreading the gospel. Church organization in the Bible, and the best of Christian history, is not about hierarchy, but about mission (Matt. 23:11; 28:19-20). Men and women are called and ordained by God to participate in this mission (Joel 2:28-29).

12. Where do gender issues fit into the big picture of creation, sin, and salvation?

    The story of humanity begins with a perfect, unified creation—a single human couple, male and female, who represent the image of God with their loving relationship. There is only one race and one social status, and the man and woman are united, rather than divided, by their gender (Gen. 2:24). When sin enters in Genesis 3, all this is shaken apart. In Genesis 9, the first mention of slavery is made (9:25), and humanity begins to be divided by social

Section I: Getting Started

status—slave and free. In Genesis 11, at the tower of Babel, the human family is separated by language, and ethnic divisions begin.

Jesus comes into this story to undo the damage of sin and to heal the divisions. In Galatians 3:26-28, Paul says that because of our status as children of God, in Christ "there is neither Jew nor Gentile, neither slave nor free, nor is there male and female, for you are all one in Christ Jesus." Nevertheless, slavery endured for thousands of years after Paul's statement, and Paul even gives instructions to Christians on how to live within the system of slavery. Racism has endured even longer. But Christians see it as their role to oppose both of them, and work for the restoration of God's created ideal of equality. Because the purpose of salvation is to restore us to God's ideal, we should seek to restore God's intention of equality between men and women as well.

Hermeneutics:
Principles to Guide Bible Study

"Do you understand what you are reading?" (Acts 8:30).

13. What is the official Seventh-day Adventist statement about the principle of giving attention to the historical and cultural context of the Bible and its different types of literature?

    Cultural context and literary style are to be considered when studying the issue of female ordination. "As far as possible ascertain the historical circumstances in which the passage was written. . . . Determine the literary type the author is using. Some biblical material is composed of parables, proverbs, allegories, psalms, and apocalyptic prophecies. . . . [M]any biblical writers presented much of their material as poetry. . . . Recognize that a given biblical text may not conform in every detail to present-day literary categories. Be cautious not to force these categories in interpreting the meaning of the biblical text. It is a human tendency to find what one is looking for, even when the author did not intend such. . . . In connection with the study of the biblical text, explore the historical and cultural factors." (Voted by General Conference Executive Committee, Annual Council, Rio de Janeiro, Brazil, Oct. 12, 1986.)

14. Is it a principle of Seventh-day Adventist biblical interpretation that the Bible must always be interpreted literally?

    No. A literalistic interpretation of the Bible leads to misunderstanding what the Bible teaches on many subjects including the subject of female ordination. The Bible itself indicates that some parts of it are highly symbolic. For example, the seven stars are seven angels and the seven lampstands are seven churches (Rev. 1:20). In addition, even parts of the Bible that are literal do have symbolic significance. For example, consider the following question. Was the earthly tabernacle built by Israel literal or symbolic? Evidently it was literal, being built by humans (Ex. 25:8). At the same time, it was symbolic of the heavenly sanctuary built by God (Heb. 8:1-2). The Bible itself explains its symbols and the context

Section I: Getting Started

of a biblical statement provides pointers to the principles of God's word and its literal or symbolic meaning.

15. Do supporters of women's ordination need to reject the Seventh-day Adventist principles for interpreting the Bible, replacing them with the higher critical method?

    No. We all reject *higher criticism,* a title Ellen White and others used for a brand of Bible scholarship popular in liberal circles in her time. Among other things, it analyzed passages of the Bible to find evidence of editing and later authorship as a way to deny predictive prophecy. Higher criticism downplays, if not outright denies, divine authorship of Scripture.

    Support for female ordination in the Adventist Church should be based on a high view of Scripture. There is no need to discredit or downplay the authority of the Bible in order to believe God calls women equally to ministry. The story of Creation, the themes of equality and redemption, and the many biblical examples of women serving in roles remarkable in their time and culture all support God's inclusive call to ministry.

    Proponents of women's ordination, when studying the text of Scripture, seek to understand what the author intended by looking at the specific words of the passage, then the literary type and the context of the passages around it, then the specific situation which it addresses, and finally the historical and cultural context, and its place in the narrative of scripture. The most profound act of respect for the biblical text is to study for what it actually means, and not for what the reader would like it to mean.

16. Do biblical writers support the principle of taking into consideration the different cultures and backgrounds of the persons to whom the Bible is addressed?

    The biblical writers do support this principle. When Paul addressed the eclectic listeners in the public square at Athens, he adapted his message to the culture and background of his audience. As a result, some joined him and became believers (Acts 17). Similarly, in his letter to the church in Corinth, Paul writes: "To the Jews I became as a Jew, that I might win Jews; to those who are under the law, as under the law, that I might win those who

Questions and Answers About Women's Ordination

are under the law; to those who are without law, as without law (not being without law toward God, but under law toward Christ), that I might win those who are without law; to the weak I became as weak, that I might win the weak. I have become all things to all men, that I might by all means save some. Now this I do for the gospel's sake, that I may be partaker of it with you" (1 Cor. 9:20-23).

17. Does Paul practice this principle of cultural sensitivity when he teaches on men and women in ministry?

Yes. Paul presents his principle of cultural sensitivity to Jews, Greeks, and Christians just before he addresses the subject of men and women in ministry (1 Cor. 11:1-16). Paul introduced his counsel to men and women as follows: "Give no offense, either to the Jews or to the Greeks or to the church of God, just as I also please all men in all things, not seeking my own profit, but the profit of many, that they may be saved" (10:32-33).

18. How should the fact that God is generally described as masculine impact our understanding of gender relationships and roles?

Although most images for God are masculine, there are certainly feminine images for God as well. God says: "Can a woman forget her nursing child, and not have compassion on the son of her womb? Surely they may forget, yet I will not forget you" (Isa. 49:15). "As one whom his mother comforts, so I will comfort you; and you shall be comforted in Jerusalem" (66:13). Jesus said: "How often I wanted to gather your children together, as a hen gathers her chicks under her wings, but you were not willing!" (Matt. 23:37).

19. Do the Bible writers sometimes use the masculine gender to refer to men and women?

Yes. Men and women are referred to as Adam/man. "This is the written account of Adam's line. When God created man, he made him in the likeness of God. He created them male and female and blessed them. And when they were created, he called them 'man'" (Gen. 5:1-2, NIV). Similarly, the masculine term *brother* sometimes

Section I: Getting Started

includes men and women. "If your brother, a Hebrew man, or a Hebrew woman, is sold to you and serves you six years, then in the seventh year you shall let him go free from you" (Deut. 15:12).

20. When the Bible does not explicitly tell us that a reference to men includes women, can the biblical principles apply also to women?

    Yes. Paul writes: "I desire therefore that the men pray everywhere, lifting up holy hands, without wrath and doubting" (1 Tim. 2:8). In principle, this instruction to men may be applied to women so that they are also to pray in a similar way. In the same way, while men are addressed in the Ten Commandments, this law is also for women. The law that states that "You shall not covet your neighbor's wife" (Ex. 20:17) applies to both genders. Applied to women, we would say: "You shall not covet your neighbor's husband."

21. When the Bible does not explicitly tell us that a reference to women includes men, can the biblical principles apply also to men?

    Yes. Paul writes: "In like manner also, that the women adorn themselves in modest apparel, with propriety and moderation, not with braided hair or gold or pearls or costly clothing, but, which is proper for women professing godliness, with good works" (1 Tim. 2:9-10). In principle, this instruction to women may be applied to men so that they are also to adorn themselves modestly.

22. Are all the practices mentioned in the Bible required practices for those who follow biblical principles?

    Not every practice mentioned in the Bible is normative for Christians. The practice of polygamy, although it appears among the Old Testament kings (2 Sam. 12:8), is not prescribed practice for Christians today. The sanctuary offerings (Heb. 10:1), the Nazarite vow (Num. 6:2. 21), and circumcision (1 Cor. 7:19), although prescribed by God, are not required of Christians. Ephesians 6, written to a culture with slavery, gives instructions for the relationship between slaves and masters. Yet it is clear that slavery is not part of God's ideal. The ethical and spiritual principles found in these legislations are still valid for us.

Questions and Answers About Women's Ordination

23. How do you know when a practice mentioned in the Bible is required by God for all time?

   Sometimes the Bible tells us that a practice it mentions is no longer required. This is the case with the practice of circumcision (Rom. 2:26, 28-29; 1 Cor. 7:19; Gal. 5:6; 6:15). At other times, there are no explicit instructions about whether a biblical practice is universal—that is, for all times and all places. For example, there is nothing in the text of 1 Corinthians 11 that would say whether the required head adornment for women is universal or not. Yet we have not taken this advice as binding for us today. Sometimes the underlying principle would require a significantly different action in one's culture today than in the culture of those for whom the biblical book was written. The only safe way is to study the passage to discover the underlying principle(s) that the biblical author is emphasizing. For example, the principles in 1 Corinthians 11 are the need to show honor (11:4-5) and to not give offense to others (10:32) by violating the generally accepted norms of society in our dress (11:6). In addition, when we compare scripture with scripture we also learn that honor should not only flow from the wife to the husband. The husband is also to honor his wife (1 Pet. 3:7). These principles are universal, but the specific application of the principles does vary in different cultures.

24. If we interpret the Bible as allowing the ordination of women, doesn't that open the way for interpreting it as allowing almost anything?

   Other related and very important questions are the following: Does the Bible prescribe female ordination or does it not? Does the Bible prohibit female ordination or does it not? Allowing what the Bible does not prescribe or prohibit does not open the way for an "anything goes" approach. As the rule of faith, the Bible gives us principles that guide us in deciding what to allow and what not to allow.

25. If we interpret the Bible as allowing for the ordination of women, doesn't that open the way for the church adopting a liberal agenda based on non-biblical principles?

Section I: Getting Started

Each person's interpretation of the Bible is impacted by their personal worldview, even those who embrace a literalist approach to Scripture. When the Bible doesn't seem to offer a clear, indisputable directive on a subject, we use a principle-based approach to Bible study that considers similar or related examples in Scripture. Bible interpretation is not a mathematical science, but is dependent on the guidance of the Spirit that leads to all truth (John 16:13). Following biblical principles does not require following a liberal agenda.

The issue of female ordination is a matter of practical policy rather than moral principle. Moral principles are general moral rules of conduct that last forever, regardless of time or place. Policies are how the principle is carried out in a particular circumstance. For instance, modesty is a principle. Wearing bonnets might have been a way to show modesty in the 19th century, but wearing bonnets is not a timeless principle—it is a policy for a particular time.

26. What do we do when the Bible neither prescribes a specific practice nor prohibits a specific practice?

While there are examples of human ordination in the Bible, the inspired word does not prescribe or prohibit the human ordination of women. In order to decide whether to practice female ordination, we have to look at basic principles taught in the Bible. We do this with many other matters. The Bible doesn't explicitly forbid smoking, but on the basis of the biblical principle of the body as the temple of God's Spirit (1 Cor. 6:19) we teach against smoking. On the other hand, the Bible doesn't explicitly command a wedding ceremony or a marriage license, but in our culture that is the way we apply the biblical principle of the importance and permanence of marriage (Gen. 2:24; Eph. 5:31).

---

1. Unless otherwise indicated, all Bible texts are from the New King James Version.

Section II:
The Old Testament

Creation

*"He created them male and female, . . .
and called them Mankind [Adam]" (Gen. 5:2).*

27. Does the Creation account in Genesis indicate that a male pastor is more suitable as the image of God than a female pastor?

    No. "God said, 'Let Us make man in Our image, according to Our likeness.' . . . So God created man in His own image; in the image of God He created him; male and female He created them" (Gen. 1:26-27).

28. Does the fact that woman was created after man indicate that women should not be pastors because men are superior to women and rulers over women?

    The Genesis story of Creation never suggests that the order of creation indicates that women are inferior. In fact, in the whole Creation story, the movement is always toward the higher creation—thus, mankind is created after the animals, who are created after the fish and birds, which are created after the plants. If Creation order were to be an indication of rulership, one would have to conclude that the woman was to rule the man. But this is not the case since man and woman are presented as two parts of the same complex creation act, as the woman is made from a piece of the already created man. Together they are the climax of God's creative action.

29. Does the fact that woman was created after man indicate that women should not be pastors because only men are intended to rule over the rest of the creation?

    No. God commissioned the man and the woman together to exercise dominion over the creation. "God said, 'Let Us make man in Our image, according to Our likeness; let them have dominion over the fish of the sea, over the birds of the air, and over the cattle, over all the earth and over every creeping thing that creeps on the earth.' So God created man in His own image; in the image of God He created him; male and female He created them. Then

Questions and Answers About Women's Ordination

God blessed them, and God said to them, 'Be fruitful and multiply; fill the earth and subdue it; have dominion over the fish of the sea, over the birds of the air, and over every living thing that moves on the earth'" (Gen. 1:26-28).

30. Does the fact that the woman is derived from the man mean that women should not be pastors because men are superior to women in some way?

Woman is no more subordinate to man because she was made from his rib than man is subordinate to the earth, since he was made of the ground. The raw material came from the man in order to show that the woman is the same sort of creature as he, which the man recognizes in his statement in Genesis 2:23. And though the material comes from the man, it is God who does the creating.

This is in full harmony with Genesis 2, where their creation is given in more detail. The life-giving breath of God has already made man into a living being (2:7) when the woman is formed from his body (2:21, 22). The woman, therefore, received her life from the same breath of life from which the man received his. His exclamation that she is "bone of my bones and flesh of my flesh" (2:23) is an acknowledgment of their sameness. Rather than suggesting a hierarchy, the Creation account shows us the unity of the new human family.

31. How can men and women be equally involved in pastoral ministry when God created men and women different from each other?

Men and women are different but equal. This is indicated in the concept of one flesh. They were created from one flesh and through marriage they become one flesh. "And the LORD God caused a deep sleep to fall on Adam, and he slept; and He took one of his ribs, and closed up the flesh in its place. Then the rib which the LORD God had taken from man He made into a woman, and He brought her to the man. And Adam said: 'This is now bone of my bones and flesh of my flesh; she shall be called Woman, because she was taken out of Man.' Therefore a man shall leave his father and mother and be joined to his wife, and they shall become one flesh" (Gen. 2:21-24).

Section II: The Old Testament

32. Are women precluded from pastoral ministry because of role distinctions instituted by God at creation?

    No. All the roles mentioned in the biblical Creation account are shared roles. First, God says, "Let them rule over the fish of the sea and the birds of the air, over the livestock, over all the earth, and over all the creatures that move along the ground" (Gen. 1:26). Second, He tells both male and female together, "Be fruitful and increase in number; fill the earth and subdue it. Rule over the fish of the sea and the birds of the air and over every living creature that moves on the ground" (1:28, NIV). Clearly, in the case of the command to procreate, there is some difference in their functions, but the task is shared, and belongs to them both. The differences require them to work together in ruling and multiplying. The same cooperation is needed in pastoral ministry.

33. Does the fact that woman was created as a helper indicate inequality with man in the exercise of dominion and, therefore, in the exercise of pastoral ministry?

    No. "The Lord God said, 'It is not good that man should be alone; I will make him a helper comparable to him'" (Gen. 2:18). In the English language, a helper is often an assistant or a subordinate, but the Hebrew word used here has no such implication. The term *comparable* indicates that the woman was a helper equal to, corresponding to, and face to face with the man. She is the corresponding piece to the man, of the same kind as him. The word *helper* does not indicate any kind of inferior or subordinate relationship. Rather, it indicates a beneficial and complementary relationship. Most of the times when the word *helper* is used in the Bible, it is God who is being called a Helper. Even though God is superior in every way, the psalmist writes: "God is my helper" (Psalm 54:4).

34. Is the participation of women in pastoral ministry limited by the fact that the man is the one to whom God gives the instructions about the Tree of Knowledge of Good and Evil?

    God tells the man about the Tree, merely because he needs to know about the danger in the garden right away—before the woman is created (Gen. 2:8-17). This does not indicate that God

Questions and Answers About Women's Ordination

gives instructions to women only through men. In fact, God often gives instruction to men through women (Ex. 15:20; Judg. 4:4; 2 Kings 22:14; Acts 21:9; Joel 2:28; Acts 2:17).

35. Is the participation of women in pastoral ministry limited by the fact that the man is the one who names the animals?

There is no indication in Genesis that the naming of the animals indicates male rulership. Rather, the man and the woman are part of the same story, and both are given dominion (Gen. 1:26-28). Through Adam's naming of male and female animals, God is creating the sense of need in the man, so that when he sees the woman, he will immediately recognize that she is the solution to his lack (2:19-25).

36. Doesn't the fact that the man names the woman show that he is exercising authority over her and that her pastoral role is limited?

The man's statement in Genesis 2:23 is not an act of unilateral authority, but of recognition—he sees right away that, unlike the animals which he had named, this creature is the same as him. In fact, she is a part of him—"bone of my bones and flesh of my flesh." He is saying precisely that they are equivalent, made of the same stuff. This act is not comparable to naming the animals. It is a recognition that she is his equivalent and partner. The man immediately recognizes that this is what he needs—this companion is right for him.

In the Bible, the act of naming, even when it occurs after the Fall, does not necessarily show authority over the one named. Throughout the Bible, God names men, and men and women name God (Gen. 16:13). In each case, they are discerning some part of the other's character or identity, rather than exercising power over them.

37. What is the significance of the lack of personal names before the Fall for the shared ministry of men and women?

Before the Fall, the first humans are mostly referred to as the man and the woman, with a couple of uses of the name Adam.

Section II: The Old Testament

Although it is the man who is called Adam, the name belongs to the woman as well, as its literal meaning is "humankind." Genesis records: "This is the book of the genealogy of Adam. In the day that God created man, He made him in the likeness of God. He created them male and female, and blessed them and called them Mankind in the day they were created" (5:1-2). The man's designation of her as woman is a statement that she is literally a part of himself (2:23). After the Fall, when the man names his wife Eve, this is an act of separation—an acknowledgment of division in the human family (3:20).

38. Doesn't there have to be subordination in the human family at creation and in ministry if they are made in the image of the triune God—Father, Son, and Holy Spirit?

No. Some have suggested that Jesus holds a subordinate role to the Father within the Trinity, and that therefore, subordination and hierarchy must have been part of God's original plan of humankind as the image of God. It is true that during Jesus' time on earth we see Him submitting Himself to the will of the Father, as in His prayer in Gethsemane (Luke 22:42). However, it is faulty to use the Incarnation as a pattern for the eternal relationships in the Trinity. During His time on earth, Jesus was subject to human limitations and surrounded by human temptation. Having limited Himself for His mission, He would have to rely fully on His Father, and trust the Father's leading. At the same time, this obedience does not give any indication of inequality in Their eternal relationship. In fact, even during the incarnation, "in Him [Christ] dwells all the fullness of the Godhead" (Col. 2:9).

The Bible presents the persons in the Godhead as sharing mutual authority and mutual submission among Themselves. The Father "has put [*hupotassō*] all things under His [Christ's] feet" (1 Cor. 15:27). In turn, Christ submits authority "when He delivers the kingdom to God the Father, when He puts an end to all rule and all authority and power" (15:24). The Father's submission of authority to Christ does not undermine the Father's authority since "when all things are made subject [*hupotassō*] to Him, then the Son Himself will also be subject to Him who put [*hupotassō*] all things under Him, that God may be all in all" (15:28).

Questions and Answers About Women's Ordination

Similarly, in John 14:16, the Spirit goes where Jesus sends, and in Mark 1:12, Jesus goes where the Spirit sends. The proposal of "lesser gods" in the Trinity resembles polytheism, while the Bible emphasizes the oneness of God (Deut. 6:4).

Sin and Salvation

"From the beginning it was not so" (Matt. 19:8).

39. Does the order of God's communication with man and woman after sin indicate that only men are to be pastoral leaders?

    No. The conversation between God, the man, the woman, and the serpent is written in poetry, and the order follows a structure common in Hebrew literature. In this structure, called a chiasm, the emphasis is in the center. We can see this when God first addresses the man, then the women, then the serpent, the woman, and finally the man again (Gen. 3:9-19). The center and focus of this passage is the promise ironically contained in the address to Satan. God says, "I will put enmity between you and the woman, and between your offspring and hers; he will crush your head, and you will strike his heel" (3:15, NIV). It is Jesus, who is called the woman's offspring, who is the center of this conversation, and His promised triumph over the serpent is the focal point of the message.

40. Did male-female relations change after sin in a way that limits the participation of women in pastoral ministry?

    The most significant change after sin is the man and woman's separation from each other. Even before God arrives, they begin to separate. They see suddenly that they are naked, and try to cover themselves. Although this is an expression of their personal sense of shame, it hides them from each other. When God arrives to address them in Genesis 3:8, they both excuse their own choices and blame someone else. "Then the man said, 'The woman whom You gave to be with me, she gave me of the tree, and I ate.' And the LORD God said to the woman, 'What is this you have done?' The woman said, 'The serpent deceived me, and I ate'" (3:12-13).

41. Did God create Adam to "rule over" Eve, indicating a limited role for women in pastoral ministry?

    No. At creation, both man and woman are told to rule over the creation (Gen. 1:26-28). Later, as God explains to the first humans the results of their sins, He tells the woman of her separation

Questions and Answers About Women's Ordination

from her husband that will lead to his rule over her. "To the woman He said: 'I will greatly multiply your sorrow and your conception; in pain you shall bring forth children; your desire shall be for your husband, and he shall rule over you'" (3:16). This rule is part of the curse following sin and is closely associated with the pain sin brought to men and women. The term in Hebrew is the same for the woman's pain in childbearing as for the man's painful toil working the ground (3:17-19).

Instead of occupying the same plane, as they had previously, the man will now rule above his wife. The accuracy of God's pronouncement is clear from the very first verse after God's words, where Adam gives his wife a separate name, making her identity separate from his (3:20). What God intended to be a provisional blessing to save the unity of the home descended swiftly into distortions of patriarchy that can be seen in the rest of the stories of Genesis.

42. Does the Fall then set the standard for Christian male-female relations, including their relations in pastoral ministry?

No. What the Fall means for Christian men and women today must be decided in light of the teaching of the Bible concerning where we stand in salvation history. The curses in Genesis are not God's first or final word on His will for the relationships between men and women. As far as is possible, we should seek to follow the principles embedded in the intentions of God for human beings at creation. Jesus expressed this principle in connection with the laws of divorce given after the Fall. "He said to them, 'Moses, because of the hardness of your hearts, permitted you to divorce your wives, but from the beginning it was not so'" (Matt. 19:8). In addition, "He answered and said to them, 'Have you not read that He who made them at the beginning "made them male and female," and said, "For this reason a man shall leave his father and mother and be joined to his wife, and the two shall become one flesh"? So then, they are no longer two but one flesh. Therefore what God has joined together, let not man separate'" (19:4-6).

43. Are women precluded from pastoral ministry because of

Section II: The Old Testament

Eve's role in the first sin and because of God's "curses" following the Fall?

No. Many biblical and historical examples show women in ministry and leadership (Ex. 15:20; Judg. 4:4; 2 Kings 22:14; Acts 21:9; Joel 2:28; Acts 2:17). When it comes to the curses—the consequences of the Fall—we note that the purpose of the people of God is to counter these curses by being a blessing. This is clear in the call of Abraham, the father of the people of God, to be a blessing to the nations (Gen. 12:1-3). As a church, we are to model the original gender equality established by God at creation, before the Fall. This is exemplified by the reversal of the "curse" of Genesis 3:16 in the Song of Songs, where the husband's desire is to the wife just as much as the wife's desire is to the husband (7:10).

The curses describe results of sin. They are consequences, not necessarily divine commands for what we are to do. In a selfishly dominated world, for instance, males have sometimes used their physical power to oppress women. We don't have to replicate that oppression, just as we don't have to force women to bear children with pain, but are allowed to ease that pain.

Precedents

"You shall be to Me a kingdom of priests" (Ex. 19:6).

44. Is female pastoral ministry supported by the Old Testament example of a female judge?

    Yes. "Now Deborah, a prophetess, the wife of Lapidoth, was judging Israel at that time. And she would sit under the palm tree of Deborah between Ramah and Bethel in the mountains of Ephraim. And the children of Israel came up to her for judgment" (Judg. 4:4-5). The judges participated in a pastoral or shepherding function since the Bible refers to rulers as shepherds (2 Sam. 5:2; Prov. 8:16). In addition, female shepherds are mentioned in the Bible such as Rachel (Gen. 29:9) and Zipporah (Ex. 2:16). The term *shepherd* also implies authority since kings are also shepherds (Psalm 78:70-71; Eze. 37:24; Mic. 5:2-4).

45. Are women precluded from pastoral ministry because Isaiah mentions the tragic woe when women lead God's people in an oppressive way?

    No. The tragedy and woe is when even women and children rule oppressively (Isa. 3:12). Such oppressive rule by men would also be a tragic woe (1 Sam. 8:5-18).

46. Was the all-male Levitical priesthood God's choice from the time of creation, showing that women have limited roles in pastoral ministry?

    With regard to the priesthood, it is important to recognize that Moses presents the Garden of Eden as the first sanctuary, and uses technical terms for the work of the priesthood (*'avad* + *shamar*) to describe the work of both Adam and Eve; they were appointed officiating priests in the Garden of Eden before the Fall (cf. Gen. 2:15 with Num. 18:3-7). Further explicit technical terms for priesthood (*labash* + *ketonet*) in Gen. 3:21 (cf. Lev. 8:7, 13) show that this priesthood of both Adam and Eve was reconfirmed as such after the Fall.

47. Was the all-male Levitical priesthood God's first choice for the nation of Israel?

Section II: The Old Testament

God's original plan was that *all* Israel be a "kingdom of priests" (Ex. 19:6). This was not just a corporate function of offering salvation to the surrounding nations, but the priesthood involved the call for all Israel—men and women—to come up on the mountain, to the place on the mountain which was equivalent to the Holy Place in the sanctuary, where only the priests could enter. Because of Israel's failure to follow God's invitation (Deut. 5:5), and their sin in the worship of the golden calf (Ex. 32), an alternate plan was given in which even most men were also excluded—except for one family in one tribe in Israel. Yet in the New Testament the Gospel restores God's original plan. Not a few male priests, but once more the "priesthood of *all* believers" (1 Pet. 2:5, 9; Rev. 1:6; 5:10; 20:6).

48. Why were women included in prophetic, religious, and social ministries in Old Testament times, but excluded from serving as priests?

The Bible does not say why women were excluded from the priesthood. To assume it is because they are unfit for spiritual leadership is not reasonable, however, because of the role of women as prophets during the same time period. It may have been a protection against abuses, as priestesses in the religions of the neighboring nations usually served a sexual role. It may have been because of the ceremonial uncleanness caused by a woman's menstrual cycle, which would exclude her from entering the sanctuary for portions of the month. It may also have been simply that female priests, who worked together regularly with men, would have been impractical in such a patriarchal culture.

49. Were women allowed to be prophets because prophets had limited authority that does not include pastoral authority?

No. The large degree of authority belonging to a prophet is evident in that God says: "I will put my words in his mouth" (Deut. 18:18). This extensive authority is also present in prophetesses since "Deborah, a prophetess" "was judging" Israel (Judg. 4:4). And the judges participated in a pastoral or shepherding function since the Bible refers to rulers as shepherds (2 Sam. 5:2; Prov. 8:16). This authority is also evident when a king of Israel sends the

Questions and Answers About Women's Ordination

priest to seek the advice of a prophetess (2 Kings 22:12-20).

50. Does the fact that the pastor is in some ways like a priest and a prophet prevent women from serving as pastors?

    Modern ministers are even more like the Old Testament prophet than like the priest, as their job is to proclaim God's Word to the people. They also resemble the priest in the fact that they are facilitating public worship. At the same time, the major priestly function of representing the people before God (as common people could not enter the sanctuary) is unnecessary because every believer is meant to be a priest, called to serve and represent God to others (1 Pet. 2:9). The ultimate model for Christian ministry is Christ (1 Pet. 2:25). He is the King-Priest of the Melchizedek priesthood (Heb. 7) and He makes us to be kings and priests with Him (Rev. 1:6; 5:10).

Section III:
The New Testament

Creation

"As the woman came from man, even so man also comes through woman" (1 Cor. 11:12).

51. Does the creation order allow for women to exercise the leadership function of the gift of prophecy in public worship?

    Yes. In 1 Corinthians, Paul uses creation order to address the issue of head adornment. He does not use it to indicate any difference between men and women in ministry function. "Every man praying or prophesying, having his head covered, dishonors his head. But every woman who prays or prophesies with her head uncovered dishonors her head. . . . For a man . . . is the image and glory of God; but woman is the glory of man. For man is not from woman, but woman from man. Nor was man created for the woman, but woman for the man. . . . Nevertheless, neither is man independent of woman, nor woman independent of man, in the Lord. For as woman came from man, even so man also comes through woman; but all things are from God" (1 Cor. 11:4-5, 7-9, 11-12).

52. Does the creation order include the process of woman coming from man as well as man coming from women?

    Yes. Procreation is part of the creation order. While the first woman was created out of man, men are also procreated through women. Paul expressed this comprehensive understanding of the creation order as follows. "Neither is man independent of woman, nor woman independent of man, in the Lord. For as woman came from man, even so man also comes through woman; but all things are from God" (1 Cor. 11:11-12).

53. Does the fact that the man is the image of God mean that a woman cannot also be the image of God in pastoral ministry?

    No. Paul does write that "a man ... is the image and glory of God; but woman is the glory of man" (1 Cor. 11:7). This does not indicate that the woman cannot be in the image of God, as well as being the glory of the man. To say that a woman is not created in the image of God would set Paul against the Bible, which states that "God created man in His own image; in the image of God He created him; male and female He created them" (Gen 1:27). Moreover, since woman is the glory of man, then man is not the glory of God without the glory of the woman (1 Cor. 11:7).

54. Because Adam was created first, does Paul then conclude that a woman cannot exercise spiritual leadership authority?

No. Paul uses the fact that "Adam was first formed, then Eve" (1 Tim. 2:13) to illustrate the importance of women and men respecting each other's authority. The fact that Adam was formed first by God illustrates the principle that the authority of men is to be respected. At the same time, the fact that Eve was also formed by God illustrates that the authority of women is also to be respected. What Paul illustrates here concerning the authority of men and women, he explicitly states in another of his letters as follows. "The wife does not have authority over her own body, but the husband does. And likewise the husband does not have authority over his own body, but the wife does" (1 Cor. 7:4).

Paul's reference to the order of creation and the Fall was meant to counter the influence of false teachings that had led believing women in Ephesus to act in ways that were seen as domineering to men in general, and their husbands in particular. To demonstrate that such behavior has no place within the church, Paul appeals to the equality of men and women that is found in the Creation account. The fact that Adam was created first does not indicate that women are somehow inferior to men. If such "first-then" terminology indicates anything more than a sequence of time, it would mean that the animals were created to be superior to humans—which is obviously not the case. The order of creation in Genesis 2 moves from incompleteness to completeness, rather, with the creation of woman as the climax and equal of Adam (Gen. 2:1-25). It is just this point that Paul wants the women in Ephesus to remember. Woman was not created to rule over man; she was created to be his equal and loving partner (1:27-28).

Section III: The New Testament

55. Does Paul's use of the Old Testament to allow for women in ministry contradict the original meaning of the Old Testament?

    No. New Testament writers, like modern preachers, often use Old Testament stories or texts to support newer applications. No matter how appropriate the later application, the original story continues to mean what it originally meant. For example, Moses said not to muzzle an ox while it is treading grain. There is no indication Moses intended this to apply to anything other than real four-legged oxen. Yet Paul appealed to this law of Moses to argue that ministers should be paid by those they serve. It is a legitimate argument, but it does not change the meaning of what Moses said. Likewise, it is clear in the Creation story that Adam and Eve were created equal, and however Paul used the Creation story does not change its meaning.

Sin and Salvation

"There is neither male nor female for you are all one in Christ Jesus" (Gal. 3:28).

56. Can a man who has been deceived in sin become qualified to teach the gospel?

    Yes. Paul presents himself in 1 Timothy 1:12-16 as a representative pattern of one who was saved (1:15-16) through "the grace of our Lord" "with faith and love" (1:14) and then called to Christian ministry. He writes: "I thank Christ ... who has enabled me ... putting me into the ministry, although I was formerly a blasphemer ... ignorantly in unbelief [lacking faith]" (1:12-13). After being converted from blasphemy, Paul "was appointed a preacher and an apostle," and "a teacher" "in faith and truth" (2:7).

57. Can a woman who has been deceived in sin become qualified to teach the gospel?

    Yes. The fact that Eve was deceived into transgression illustrates the principle that women need to learn in silence (peace) and self-control. At the same time, this illustration is representative since men also need to learn in the same way. Similarly, in a letter to the Corinthians, Paul uses Eve as an illustration applicable to both men and women as follows. "I fear, lest somehow, as the serpent deceived Eve by his craftiness, so your minds may be corrupted from the simplicity that is in Christ" (2 Cor. 11:3).

    The fact that Eve was deceived into sin in Eden does not disqualify women from teaching, even as Paul was not disqualified though he was formerly a blasphemer (1 Tim. 1:12-16). Paul was saved by Christ in faith and love (2:7). Similarly, women may be "saved in [the] childbearing [*tes tecnogonias*] if they continue in faith and love" (2:15). In this way they become qualified to be "teachers of good things" (Titus 2:3).

    In light of the impact heretical ideas were having upon the women in Ephesus, Paul's allusion to the story of Eve and the Fall was meant to serve as a vivid warning about the dangers of listening and being influenced by false teachers. The story of Eve's involvement in the Fall illustrated in the strongest of terms just how

Section III: The New Testament

tragic the results could be for the church if the women in Ephesus continued in their course. Just as Eve had rejected God's word and authority over her life, the women in Ephesus would be guilty of following after the words of the false teachers rather than following God.

58. Does Paul's statement about equality in Galatians 3:28 apply only to equality in salvation, or does it also apply to equality in pastoral ministry?

Paul teaches that "There is neither Jew nor Greek, there is neither slave nor free, there is neither male nor female; for you are all one in Christ Jesus" (Gal. 3:28). One must allow Paul to indicate just what kind of equality he means is bestowed on us because we are all one. In Galatians 2, just two chapters before, Paul points out his dispute with Peter because the latter stopped eating with the Gentiles, calling it "hypocrisy" (2:13), and saying he was "not acting in line with the truth of the gospel" (2:14). Paul believes the equality of Jew and Gentile is not just about salvation, but is social equality as well. In the same context he refers to the importance of remembering the poor (2:10). There is no reason to believe he thinks any differently about the equality between men and women, or slave and free, which he mentions in the same context as ethnic equality.

The purpose of Christ's ministry is salvation, redemption and restoration. He came to break down the barriers of alienation that sin had caused between people, and as far as possible, restore the Eden ideal. This meant breaking down the dividing wall between Jew and Gentile, but also included breaking down the barriers in the male-female relationship. Physical, social, and emotional differences remain between men and women, of course, but they are fully equal in Christ. This means that neither stands over the other or controls the other. They have equal access to God and to ministering for Him. Both are to submit mutually to each other out of reverence for Christ (Eph. 5:21).

59. Does the submission of wives to husbands as to Christ in Ephesians 5:22 disqualify women from pastoral ministry?

No. Husbands and wives are to be "submitting to one another in the fear of God" (Eph. 5:21). This is the context in which Paul instructs: "Wives, submit to your own husbands, as to the Lord" (5:22). There are significant differences between this relationship and the relationship among members of the church including leaders. The husband's relation to his wife illustrates Christ's relation to the church. Yet, no man other than Christ is the head of the church. "For the husband is head of the wife, as also Christ is head of the church; and He is the Savior of the body" (5:23). He is the only "head of the body" (Col. 1:18) and the only "head over all things to the church" (1:22). Paul also writes: "I have betrothed you to one husband, that I may present you as a chaste virgin to Christ" (2 Cor. 11:2). This makes it evident that the pastor is not the head of the church.

60. Why did the issue of gender roles get so much attention in the New Testament?

Paul's statements about women in the church and the home may be seen as evidence that the Christian faith was coming into conflict with the patriarchy of the time. A faith that taught that all people were equal in Christ, and that women were accepted in public worship and even evangelism was a revolutionary and freeing idea. Paul desired to protect the Christian revolution from being misunderstood. Therefore, he urges believers to respect the social structure in which they live where they could do so without compromising their faith. He focuses the believers' attention on what is beneficial and will increase their witness to those around them.

61. How can we make the egalitarianism of Galatians 3:28 a reality in our practice of pastoral ministry?

The unique characteristic of Christian leadership is submission to the needs of others. This characteristic reflects the nature of God Himself as revealed in Christ (Phil. 2:5-11). God's challenge to us is to create a loving community based on unselfish mutual service, helping us by our fellowship to exemplify His kingdom on earth and prepare people to live for eternity. God's vision for us is to take the world back to Eden (Matt. 19:4-8; 2 Cor. 5:17), countering the results of sin and reflecting Jesus Christ by never abusing

Section III: The New Testament

power in our social relationships (Matt. 20:25-28). His kingdom is to be among us (Luke 17:21).

The only way to reach that goal is for each of us to submit to the crucified Savior, known to us from the way the Holy Spirit portrays Him in the Bible. Only then are we able to put aside our personal and culturally conditioned prejudices, gender biases included. This is echoed by a statement in the Adventist Church's Fundamental Belief No. 14: "We are all equal in Christ, who by one Spirit has bonded us into one fellowship with Him and with one another; we are to serve and be served without partiality or reservation."

Precedents

"Help these women who labored with me in the gospel" (Phil. 4:3).

62. What roles did women have during the ministry of Jesus?

    Although there were no women among the Twelve, there were certainly women among Jesus' followers who would travel to see Him, and sometimes with Him, and who gave financial and practical support to His ministry. Mark 15:40 mentions Mary Magdalene, Mary the mother of James the lesser, and Salome who followed Jesus and cared for His needs, as well as many other women from Jerusalem. Luke 8 mentions many women who followed Jesus and supported Him and His disciples from their own means. Mary, the sister of Lazarus, sat at Jesus' feet and learned from Him as would a disciple (Luke 10:42).

63. What is the significance of Jesus' appearance to women right after His resurrection?

    The first appearances Jesus made after His resurrection were to women. Because the women were the first to return to the tomb, hoping to tend to Jesus' body, they were the first to learn about the resurrection. It was Mary Magdalene, and others, who became the first messengers of the good news, the very first evangelists (Matt. 28:1-10; Mark 16:1-11; Luke 24:1-11; John 20:1-18).

64. Why were there no women among Jesus' twelve disciples?

    The Bible does not give us an explanation for why there were no women among the disciples Jesus chose to be the Twelve. Bible students have suggested a number of reasons. (1) Jesus was intentionally forming a "Representative Israel," replicating the twelve sons of Israel with the twelve apostles. (2) It would have been very difficult for men and women to live and travel together the way Jesus and His twelve disciples did during the years of His ministry. (3) Including women among the Twelve would have raised questions about the morality of Jesus and His disciples, undermining their ministry. (4) In a patriarchal society, men would be better able to travel and preach as apostles.

65. Does the absence of women among Jesus' twelve disciples

Section III: The New Testament

indicate that women are excluded from pastoral ministry?

The twelve disciples were not only exclusively male, they also included no slave, no freed slave, and no Gentile or non-Jew. If Gentiles can participate in pastoral ministry, then the fact that there were not women among the Twelve does not exclude them from such ministry.

Women were mentioned as following Jesus, but to travel full time with Him among the Twelve would have been viewed with suspicion and disapproval. It would have raised questions of propriety about Jesus as well as the other disciples. Including female disciples would have undermined the ministry of Jesus. It appears that His choice was in deference to the culture of the day.

Compared with, for instance, the Pharisaic party, Jesus was unique in His positive attitude toward women—and women were the first to proclaim the message of the resurrected Savior. From the outset, these factors positioned the early Christian church as a far more egalitarian movement than was the custom.

66. Are there any Bible precedents of women as apostles?

Paul mentions a woman among the apostles when he writes: "Greet Andronicus and Junia, my countrymen and my fellow prisoners, who are of note among the apostles" (Rom. 16:7). The translation of this passage in Romans is debated among Bible students. Some suggest that Junia was highly regarded by the apostles rather than a highly regarded apostle. Others suggest that if an apostle is one who is sent on a mission by Christ—an apostle is a missionary—then, from this perspective, Junia could very well have been an apostle. There are many other apostles mentioned in the New Testament beyond the select group of the Twelve, such as Paul, Silas, Barnabas, and Titus. In addition, from Ephesians 4 and 1 Corinthians 12, we read that the Holy Spirit gives gifts, including apostles, to all to whom He chooses, male and female.

67. Does the Apostle Paul regard women as his helpers in ministry?

Yes. In Romans, he writes: "I commend to you Phoebe our sister, who is a servant [deacon or minister] of the church in Cenchrea,

Questions and Answers About Women's Ordination

that you may receive her in the Lord in a manner worthy of the saints, and assist her in whatever business she has need of you; for indeed she has been a helper of many and of myself also" (Rom. 16:1-2). The significance of the ministry of Phoebe is indicated by the fact that the word *helper* (*proistemi*) means to be set before or set over for the purpose of care and protection (Rom. 12:8; 1 Thess. 5:12; 1 Tim. 3:4-5, 12, 17).

68. Does Paul regard women as his fellow workers in gospel ministry?

Paul writes: "Greet Priscilla and Aquila, my fellow workers in Christ Jesus" (Rom. 16:3); "Greet Mary, who labored much for us" (16:6); "Greet Tryphena and Tryphosa, who have labored in the Lord. Greet the beloved Persis, who labored much in the Lord. Greet Rufus, chosen in the Lord, and his mother and mine" (16:12-13); "Greet Philologus and Julia, Nereus and his sister, and Olympas, and all the saints who are with them" (16:15). In Philippians, Paul writes: "I implore Euodia and I implore Syntyche to be of the same mind in the Lord. And I urge you also, true companion, help these women who labored with me in the gospel, with Clement also, and the rest of my fellow workers, whose names are in the Book of Life" (Phil. 4:2-3).

69. What is the significance of the fact that Paul regards women as his fellow workers in gospel ministry?

Paul regards his fellow workers as persons to whose ministry the church is to submit. He writes: "I urge you, brethren—you know the household of Stephanas, that it is the firstfruits of Achaia, and that they have devoted themselves to the ministry of the saints—that you also submit to such, and to everyone who works and labors with us" (1 Cor. 16:15-16).

This appeal also includes, in principle, an appeal for submission to the "women who labored with me in the gospel" (Phil. 4:3). This is because the term *fellow worker* is used to identify a person who is like Paul a representative of God. The fellow worker is not a subordinate person since Paul is also only a "fellow worker" (2 Cor. 1:24; 6:1) among the men and women through whom God works in gospel ministry.

Section III: The New Testament

70. How are the leadership roles of women described in the New Testament?

The book of Acts shows women taking roles that would have been remarkable in their first-century culture. They were prophets, such as the daughters of Philip (Acts 21:9), and host-leaders of house churches, such as Lydia and Nympha (Col. 4:15). When Saul persecuted the Christians, he targeted both men and women (Acts 9:2). Apparently the women contributed enough to the movement that he felt both must be stopped in order to halt the spread of the belief. When Priscilla and Aquila taught Apollos, her name is mentioned first, a suggestion that she was more prominent in the act of teaching (Acts 18:24-26). And Paul mentions many women and their work in his letters (Rom. 16:1-3, 6, 12-13, 15), including the women who were leaders in the church of Philippi (Phil. 4:1-3).

71. Are there any Bible precedents of women as disciples?

Yes. "These all continued with one accord in prayer and supplication, with the women and Mary the mother of Jesus, and with His brothers. And in those days Peter stood up in the midst of the disciples (altogether the number of names was about a hundred and twenty)" (Acts 1:14-15). In Acts 9:36, Dorcas is specifically described as a disciple, the one woman specifically designated as such in the New Testament.

72. Does the New Testament teach that the all-male Levitical priesthood was God's *original* plan for the priesthood?

No. The Melchizedeck priesthood preceded the Levitical priesthood and was a better priesthood. "For this Melchizedek, king of Salem, priest of the Most High God, who met Abraham returning from the slaughter of the kings and blessed him, to whom also Abraham gave a tenth part of all. . . . Now consider how great this man was, to whom even the patriarch Abraham gave a tenth. . . . And indeed those who are of the sons of Levi, who receive the priesthood, have a commandment to receive tithes. . . . But he whose genealogy is not derived from them received tithes from Abraham and blessed him who had the promises. Now beyond all

Questions and Answers About Women's Ordination

contradiction the lesser is blessed by the better. . . . Even Levi, who receives tithes, paid tithes through Abraham, so to speak, for he was still in the loins of his father when Melchizedek met him" (Heb. 7:1-10).

73. Does the New Testament teach that the all-male Levitical priesthood was God's *final* plan for the priesthood?

No. "For the [Levitical] priesthood being changed, of necessity there is also a change of the law. For He of whom these things are spoken belongs to another tribe, from which no man has officiated at the altar. For it is evident that our Lord arose from Judah, of which tribe Moses spoke nothing concerning priesthood. And it is yet far more evident if, in the likeness of Melchizedek, there arises another priest who has come, not according to the law of a fleshly commandment, but according to the power of an endless life. For He testifies: 'You are a priest forever according to the order of Melchizedek.' For on the one hand there is an annulling of the former commandment because of its weakness and unprofitableness" (Heb. 7:12-18).

74. Does the Melchizedek priesthood include men and women who are in Christ?

Yes. The Melchizedek priesthood is made up of king-priests (Heb. 7:2), and Christ "has made us kings and priests" (Rev. 1:6; 5:10). We "shall be priests of God and of Christ, and shall reign [as kings] with Him" (20:6). All men and women "who believe" (2 Pet. 2:7) are "a royal priesthood" (2:9; cf. 2:5). They are included in the Melchizedek priesthood.

The Old Testament priesthood is not the model for the New Testament Christian community. It's true that the Old Testament priests were exclusively male; they were also chosen from only one tribe, the Levites. The Levitical system included dozens of ordinances that are not to be practiced today, such as sacrificing lambs.

75. Does the biblical record of female prophets have any implications for women in pastoral ministry?

Both the Old and New Testaments indicate that God chose women to serve as prophets to His people, and as such they were

Section III: The New Testament

spokespersons of God's messages to the people. Miriam (Ex. 15:20), Deborah (Judg. 4:4), and Huldah (2 Kings 22:14) are examples in the Old Testament. The daughters of Philip are examples in the New Testament (Acts 21:9). The role of pastor in the New Testament church is closely modeled on the role of a prophet. Like the prophet, the pastor is a spokesperson for God, explaining the Word of God to the people and protecting the flock with care and supervision. This biblical image of a prophetic pastor is fulfilled by both men and women. This is the sense in which men and women will be prophets when the Spirit of God is poured out on all flesh (Joel 2:28; Acts 2:17).

76. Does Paul indicate that he expects women will have an active role in public worship?

In 1 Corinthians 11:5, Paul says that women need to have their heads covered when they pray or prophesy in public. It is clear, then, that he must not be expecting all women to keep silent at all times, because he is telling them the proper way to be dressed when they speak up. Furthermore, this instruction appears in the middle of a long discussion about relationships in the church and propriety in worship, including the Lord's Supper, and using spiritual gifts in church. While prayer may be interpreted as a private act, prophesying is done to give a message to others, and the concern for modesty reinforces that this is public ministry.

Headship

"I have betrothed you to one husband ... to Christ" (2 Cor. 11:2).

77. Are female pastors improper because male pastors function as the head of the church along with Christ?

    No. Christ is the only head of the church. He is "head over all things to the church" (Eph. 1:22). "Christ is head of the church" (5:23). "He is the head of the body, the church" (Col. 1:18). Paul also writes: "I have betrothed you to one husband, that I may present you as a chaste virgin to Christ" (2 Cor. 11:2). There are no Bible texts that even hint that the pastor, male or female, should function as the head of the church.

78. Are female pastors improper because only men grow up into Christ—the head of the church?

    No. All Christians are to "grow up in all things into Him who is the head—Christ" (Eph. 4:15). He is the head of "the whole body" in which "every part does its share" (4:16).

79. Are female pastors to be excluded because Adam's headship over the race was transferred to men in general?

    No. Adam's headship is transferred only to the incarnate Christ. "The first man Adam became a living being. The last Adam became a life-giving spirit" (1 Cor. 15:45). Both men and women are included in the first Adam and in Christ—the last Adam. "This is the book of the genealogy of Adam. In the day that God created [Adam], He made him in the likeness of God. He created them male and female, and blessed them and called them [Adam] in the day they were created" (Gen. 5:1-2). "As in Adam all die, even so in Christ all shall be made alive" (1 Cor. 15:22).

80. Are female pastors excluded because the headship of a husband-wife relationship is transferrable to church leadership?

    There is no text that would indicate there ought to be a general headship of all men over all women. Paul writes: "Let each one of you in particular so love his own wife as himself, and let the wife

Section III: The New Testament

see that she respects her husband" (Eph. 5:33). Similarly, "Let each man have his own wife, and let each woman have her own husband" (1 Cor. 7:2).

Further, even if there were a transfer of husband-wife relations to church leadership, this would call for team ministry with authority shared by men and women, paralleling the marriage relationship. Paul writes: "The wife does not have authority over her own body, but the husband does. And likewise the husband does not have authority over his own body, but the wife does" (1 Cor. 7:4). Note the fluid and shared character of authority, even in marriage, which is generally considered to be a realm of distinct roles.

81. Does the fact that the husband is head of the wife exclude a wife from ordination to pastoral ministry?

No. When Paul encourages the husband to act as a head like Christ, he is calling him to love and self-sacrifice for the best good of his wife (Eph. 5:23-30). A husband doing this will encourage his wife to use fully the gifts God has given her, and he will celebrate when the church recognizes these gifts through ordination.

82. Does the biblical concept of "head" as "authority" exclude the concept of "head" as "source"?

No. For Paul, the word *head* implies authority when Jesus is presented as "head over all things to the church" (Eph. 1:22). The meaning of this headship authority is illuminated by the statement that God "has put all things under His feet" (1 Cor. 15:27) until "He puts an end to all rule and all authority and power. For He must reign till He has put all enemies under His feet" (15:24-25).

At the same time, Paul uses the word *head* in several passages to include the concept of "source." He explains 1 Corinthians 11:3 by saying: "I want you to know that the head of every man is Christ, the head of woman is man, and the head of Christ is God.... For man is not from woman, but woman from man.... For as woman came from man, even so man also comes through woman; but all things are from God" (1 Cor. 11:3, 8, 12).

That God is the ultimate authority and source of authority is made explicit when Paul writes that "there is no authority except from God, and the authorities that exist are appointed by God" (Rom. 13:1). This is why the wife submits to her husband as to the Lord (Eph. 5:22). It is also why husbands and wives submit to each other (5:21). "The wife does not have authority over her own body, but the husband does. And likewise the husband does not have authority over his own body, but the wife does" (1 Cor. 7:4).

83. Do the different requirements for male and female head adornment signal any difference in the roles of spiritual leadership?

No. The principle behind Paul's advice would apply equally to men and women but be applied differently by men and women. "Every man praying or prophesying, having his head covered, dishonors his head. But every woman who prays or prophesies with her head uncovered dishonors her head" (1 Cor. 11:4-5). The principle that applies equally to men and women is that they should honor their heads. Neither should give offense that would damage the influence of the gospel. In that culture, a specific kind of head adornment could be used to show honor or to give offense. Paul's concern is expressed in the near context. "Give no offense, either to the Jews or to the Greeks or to the church of God, just as I also please all men in all things, not seeking my own profit, but the profit of many, that they may be saved" (10:32-33).

84. What does Paul teach on headship and submission in the family and the church?

In Ephesians 5:22-33, in the context of "submitting to one another," Paul tells wives to submit to their husbands as part of his instruction on household order (5:22). Husbands, for their part, are told to reciprocate with Christlike love (5:25). This is because the husband is head of the wife in the same way that Christ is the head of the church. This very passage, however, contradicts the idea that male headship should be applied to the church, as he clearly here says that Christ is the head of the church (5:23). Paul does not use the image of a marriage or a family for the relationship between the pastor and the rest of the church.

Section III: The New Testament

85. Do the differences between men and women exclude women from ordination as pastors?

    No. The differences between men and women are complementary within the different ways to administer or exercise of the gifts and offices ordained by God. "There are diversities of gifts, but the same Spirit. There are differences of ministries, but the same Lord. And there are diversities of activities, but it is the same God who works all in all. But the manifestation of the Spirit is given to each one for the profit of all" (1 Cor. 12:4-7).

Pastors, Elders, and Deacons

"He, Himself gave some to be ... pastors" (Eph. 4:11).

86. What are the biblical texts used by Seventh-day Adventists as the basis for our identification of three offices for which persons are ordained?

   The Seventh-day Adventist Minister's Handbook states on page 85:

   "The Scriptures distinguish three categories of ordained officers:

   "(1) the gospel minister, whose role may be seen as preaching/teaching, administering the ordinances, and pastoral care of the church (1 Tim. 4:14; 2 Tim. 4:1-5);

   "(2) the elder, who exercises oversight of a local congregation, performing some pastoral functions as well (Acts 14:23; 20:17; Titus 1:5, 9; 1 Tim. 3:2, 5);

   "(3) the deacon, to whose care the poor and the benevolent work of the congregation are entrusted (Phil. 1:1; Acts 6:1-6; 1 Tim. 3:8-13)."

87. Does the masculine term *elder* necessarily exclude women?

   No. The author of the book of Hebrews makes a representative statement in describing "the elders [who] obtained a good testimony" (Heb. 11:2) as including Sarah (11:11), Rahab (11:31), and other women (11:35). These elders were part of the general order of the people of God. These are not examples of the ministry of "elder" in the New Testament church. But these examples show that in biblical terminology, masculine language can be used to include women.

   Female elders are also mentioned in the following text: "Rebuke not an elder but entreat him as a father and the younger men as brethren; the elder women as mothers and the younger women as sisters" (1 Tim. 5:1-2, KJV). Some Bible students conclude that these elder women held some official position in church leadership

Section III: The New Testament

for various reasons. This reference to male and female elders is preceded by a reference to the council of elders (4:14). It is also followed by qualifications for elder widows (5:3-16) that are parallel with the qualifications for male elders (3:1-11). The discussion of elder widows (and the widows that are not qualified, in part, because they have not ruled well at home [5:14]) is followed by a summary statement about elders who rule well (5:17-20). Paul proceeds from the male and female elders who should not be rebuked (5:1-2) to the elders who should be rebuked (5:19-20).

Other Bible students conclude that these elders are not official elders because they are mentioned in close connection with young persons in the church. Therefore, these elders may simply be old persons. Nevertheless, even this view does not change the fact that both men and women are referred to as elders. Therefore, the term *elder* when used to refer to those who hold an official office does not automatically exclude women.

While the word *presbyteros* can designate both an older person (Philem. 9; Luke 15:25; Acts 2:17) as well as someone serving as an elder within the church (1 Tim. 4:14; 5:17), the context indicates that here Paul is describing the spirit that is to characterize a church leader's relationship with different age groups within the church. While church leaders, whether male or female, are called to treat older men and women within the church with the utmost respect, it does not meant that older individuals are beyond correction. It merely means that if correction is necessary, it is the duty of a church leader to administer correction with the same affection and concern that would be shown to one's own parents. Additionally, younger individuals within the church should be treated as if they were siblings.

88. Are women excluded from being elders and bishops because they do not have all the characteristics of a blameless person that are listed by Paul?

No. The essential qualification is that the elder be blameless. Paul lists examples of ways in which a potential elder may demonstrate blamelessness. A person does not have to possess all of the possible positive qualifications (such as being a married man) in order to be a blameless elder. The qualification of being "the husband of

Questions and Answers About Women's Ordination

one wife" (Titus 1:5-7; 1 Tim. 3:2) applies in principle to the "blameless" (1 Tim. 5:7) elder-widow (5:1-3) who is to be "the wife of one man" (5:9). The principle Paul promotes is the sexual purity of the elder, not that the elder is a married man. The elder widow is currently unmarried because her husband is dead; yet she has a blameless character. Similarly, while a male deacon is to be a blameless "husband of one wife" (3:12), the woman Phoebe has the same blameless character and therefore serves as a deacon (Rom. 16:1).

Paul indicates negative disqualifications for elder-bishops as follows: "a bishop then must be blameless" (1 Tim. 3:2), "not given to wine, not violent, not greedy for money, but gentle, not quarrelsome, not covetous" (3:3; cf. Titus 1:6-7). Again, Paul's emphasis is on the qualification of blamelessness rather than on specific ways in which a person may be disqualified. This means that an unqualified person does not have to possess all of the negative traits mentioned. For example, a person who is violent does not also have to be greedy in order to be unfit for the office of elder.

89. Isn't Paul describing elders as men where he mentions the phrase "husbands of one wife"?

No. Paul's concern is not the gender of a church leader, but rather the type of character that should define the life of a spiritual leader. This is evident for two reasons:

First, Paul does not restrict the desire to serve as an "overseer" to individuals of only the male gender. In the original Greek, as most translations indicate, Paul says that *"anyone"* who wants to serve as an overseer "desires a noble task." *Anyone* means any man or woman. If Paul had wanted to limit the ministry of an overseer to men, he could have easily restricted the meaning of the indefinite pronoun by adding a gender-specific noun or pronoun with it (as he does elsewhere; cf. 1 Tim. 5:4, 16; 1 Cor. 7:12-13, 36). In addition, no masculine pronoun occurs in Greek throughout the entire list of qualifications for the ministry of an overseer, or elder, as we say today. The terminology in the passage is gender inclusive.

Second, not only can women fulfill all of the requirements Paul sets forth for an overseer, but also none of the qualifications

Section III: The New Testament

specifically exclude women as potential candidates. The requirement that an overseer be the "husband of one wife" (or literally, "a one-woman man") also does not specifically exclude women. While this expression is gender specific, it is not gender exclusive. This is evident in the fact that Paul applies this same criterion to both male and female deacons (1 Tim. 3:8-13). It would have to apply then to the woman Phoebe, whom Paul identifies as a deacon in Romans 16:1. Thus the expression "husband of one wife" is not meant to emphasize the gender of the elder or deacon, but rather to point to the importance of sexual purity, which in Paul's day was understood in the context of a monogamous relationship. The passage no more excludes women from ministry than it does single or childless men from serving the church as overseers.

The requirement that an elder be the "husband of one wife" is what it appears to be—a requirement of monogamy. The use of the term *husband* is merely another example of Paul's use of male language. A woman, therefore, can fulfill this requirement, because she is equally able to be monogamous. We apply the principle behind this requirement, just as we would if the candidate were a single or childless man.

90. Does the fact that male elders are to be treated as fathers indicate that pastors must be men?

The first major problem with this argument is that the New Testament texts never say that elders and ministers have to be male! Nowhere in the New Testament is the elder called "the head." The text about headship in Ephesians 5:23 speaks about marriage—and certainly, we would not call the husband/head of his wife her "father." Likewise, no New Testament text calls the elder "father." Jesus as the head of the church is not compared to a father. He is our older brother and leaders of the church are rather older siblings taking responsibility. Indeed, we are advised *not* to call human leaders our "father" (see Matt. 23:8-10).

91. Why does Paul use male language when talking about the requirements for elders in 1 Timothy 3 and Titus 1?

In antiquity the "default" gender for a mixed group was always masculine. If there were a group of several women and only one

Questions and Answers About Women's Ordination

man, the language to describe the group would be masculine. Gender inclusive language is a fairly recent phenomenon and would not have been a consideration in Paul's time.

Paul's use of the male gender does not indicate whether there were women elders in his time. Masculine gender is the "default" language for inclusive description. Consider God's use of the male gender in the Ten Commandments. It is not because He assumes that in most cases the reader will be male! Similarly, Paul often addresses the early church as "brethren," even though the church may have been comprised of more women than men.

92. Are women excluded from being elders because, while members are to submit to elders, men are not to submit to women?

No. The Bible teaches that all Christians are to submit to each other (Eph. 5:21). This principle is indicated in the following appeal by Paul: "I urge you, brethren—you know the household of Stephanas, that it is the firstfruits of Achaia, and that they have devoted themselves to the ministry of the saints—that you also submit to such, and to everyone who works and labors with us" (1 Cor. 16:15-16).

Note that the submission of servant leaders to service is the basis of the appeal for submission from the rest of the church. Also, the entire household of Stephanas, presumably including women, had submitted themselves to the service of the church. The church submits to servant leaders whether they are male or female.

Jesus articulated a general principle of servant leadership when He said: "You know that the rulers of the Gentiles lord it over them, and their great men exercise authority over them. It is not this way among you, but whoever wishes to become great among you shall be your servant, and whoever wishes to be first among you shall be your slave" (Matt. 20:25-27).

In one of his letters, Peter restates this is the gospel principle of mutual submission between those who lead and those who follow: "The elders who are among you I exhort, I who am a fellow elder and a witness of the sufferings of Christ, and also a partaker of the glory that will be revealed: Shepherd the flock of God which is

Section III: The New Testament

among you, serving as overseers, not by compulsion but willingly, not for dishonest gain but eagerly; *nor as being lords over those entrusted to you*, but being examples to the flock; and when the Chief Shepherd appears, you will receive the crown of glory that does not fade away. *Likewise you younger people, submit yourselves to your elders. Yes, all of you be submissive to one another*" (1 Pet. 5:1-5, emphasis added).

93. Should there be female pastors in every local church in order for the global church to be united?

    No. The church remained united when some held circumcision to be a biblical requirement for all Christians while others saw it only as a requirement for Jews. The decision was made not to trouble the Gentile Christians (Acts 15:17) with a requirement of circumcision (15:24). Paul referred to this decision in terms of a distinction between two equally legitimate evangelistic strategies within the united church: one strategy called "the gospel for the uncircumcised" and the other called "the gospel for the circumcised" (Gal. 2:7). These are not two different gospels. Rather the one gospel is presented with sensitivity to the differences between Jews and Gentiles. The church is united today, yet we don't have similar worldwide practice on the issue of female pastors. Our unity doesn't depend on uniformity on this issue.

Teaching Authority
"Charge some that they teach no other doctrine" (1 Tim. 1:3).

94. Does Paul prohibit all women from teaching, or does he prohibit women from teaching false doctrines?

    The prohibition against women exercising authority over men in 1 Timothy 2:11-12 is part of the apostle's overall response to the malicious influence of false teachers who were undermining the faith of the believers in Ephesus (cf. 1:3-4; 18-20; 4:1-4; 6:20-21). Paul addresses the behavior of the women in Ephesus in particular because they had lost sight of the true gospel and the implication it had on how they should live as followers of Christ. Under the direction of the false teachers, these women had developed a disdain for the traditional role of women as wives and mothers (cf. 4:3; 5:9-10, 14) that led them to not only begin to dress immodestly (2:9-10; 5:6), but also to act in ways that were seen as domineering over their husbands and other men as well (2:11-12).

95. Does Paul prohibit women from the exercise of church authority, or does he prohibit women from the abuse of church authority?

    The indication that the problem was a ruling or domineering form of behavior being exercised by the women in Ephesus is found in the Greek word translated as "authority." Instead of using *exousia*, the regular word used in the New Testament for authority (e.g., Rom. 9:21; 13:3; 2 Cor. 13:10; 2 Thess. 3:9), Paul uses an extremely rare word that occurs nowhere else in the New Testament: *authenteō*. This verb has a negative element of force associated with it. It can mean "to rule/reign," and "to control" or "to dominate." Rather than exercising the normal form of authority that is associated with the office of ministry, these women were behaving in a way that was overbearing. The domineering behavior of these women was opposed to the traditionally subordinate role of women to men in the ancient Roman world. Also, their behavior was completely at odds with the spirit of Christlike love, selflessness, and mutual submission that is to define the relationship between all believers, and especially the marriage relationship

Section III: The New Testament

between Christians (Eph. 5:15-32).

96. Can women and men share authority with each other?

    Yes. "The wife does not have authority over her own body, but the husband does. And likewise the husband does not have authority over his own body, but the wife does" (1 Cor. 7:4).

97. Should men and women submit to each other?

    Yes. They should be "submitting to one another in the fear of God" (Eph. 5:21).

Silent Women

"You can all prophesy one by one, that all may learn" (1 Cor. 14:31).

98. Why does Paul tell the Corinthian women to keep silent in church?

In 1 Corinthians 14:33-35, Paul tells women to keep silent and to ask any questions they might have to their husbands at home. This passage is just a few chapters after his instruction to women to cover their heads when they pray or prophesy in public (11:4-5), and it is part of a multichapter discussion about orderly worship. Earlier in chapter 14, he speaks about the gift of tongues needing to be useful—that is, the message must be interpreted (14:4-21). Then he discusses the advantages of prophesying in contrast with the disadvantages of uninterpreted tongues (14:22-33). Further, he tells them that an unbeliever who came into the service and heard everyone speaking at once would only think they were insane (14:24). Paul's advice to prophets and to those who speak in tongues is about taking turns, speaking in order, and not talking over one another (14:26-32).

The rule about the women keeping silent, which comes directly after that, is part of the same concern. He introduces his advice about women with these words: "God is not the author of confusion but of peace" (14:33). Because the solution is women asking questions to their husbands at home (14:35), we can see that Paul is not talking about women teaching in church, but about women interrupting the service with questions—one more example of the chaos when believers talk over each other. It is this very church to whom Paul had just written that women should have their heads covered when they prophesy (11:4-5), so it is clear he means them to participate, but not—as listeners—to interrupt in a disorderly manner. He ends his instruction with the words "Let all things be done decently and in order" (14:40).

99. Does Paul instruct men as well as women to "keep silent"?

Yes. When Paul instructs that women should "keep silent [*sigaō*]" (1 Cor. 14:34), he presents a principle that applies to men and women. This is evident in the following instruction concerning the

Section III: The New Testament

one who speaks in tongues: "If there is no interpreter, let him keep silent [*siagō*] in church, and let him speak to himself and to God" (14:28). In the near context, Paul uses the neuter pronoun when he writes "if anyone speaks in a tongue" (14:27). He also refers to confusion caused by all speaking in tongues at the same time (14:23). While women are not explicitly mentioned, there is no reason to presume that they were not involved as well as the men.

Similarly, Paul addresses men and women who prophesy when he writes that "if anything is revealed to another who sits by, let the first keep silent" (14:30). Earlier in the letter Paul indicates that men and women prophesied in public Christian worship services (11:4-5). He also refers to the confusion caused when all prophesy at the same time (14:23). It is clear that Paul did not tell women to be silent just because they were not men. Men and women are allowed to speak in Christian ministry.

100. Is Paul's instruction that women "learn in silence with all submission" applicable also to men?

Yes. When Paul instructs a woman to "learn in silence [*hesuchia*] with all submission [*hupotagē*]" (1 Tim. 2:11), his teaching is applicable to men and women. He uses a Greek word for silence that he also uses to describe what the entire church should pray for—"a peaceable [*hesuchios*] life" (2:1-2). In another letter Paul advises Christian men and women to be "in quietness [*hesuchia*]" rather than being "disorderly" (1 Thess. 3:11-12). Paul also uses a Greek word for submission that he also uses to describe Christian men and women in terms of "the obedience [*hupotagē*] of your confession to the gospel of Christ" (2 Cor. 9:13).

It is important to note that before instructing the women, Paul mentions the need for "faith and a good conscience, which some having rejected, concerning the faith have suffered shipwreck, of whom are Hymenaeus and Alexander, whom I delivered to Satan that they may learn not to blaspheme" (1 Tim. 1:19-20). It is immediately after this reference to men who needed to learn that Paul instructs concerning prayer for a peaceable life (2:1-2). Then he instructs men to pray without wrath (2:8). The teaching concerning women learning in silence is simply a continuation of teaching on a principle that had already been applied to men.

Section IV: The Seventh-day Adventist Church

Ellen White

101. Does Ellen White affirm the offices of pastor, elder, and deacon?

> "The responsibility of representing Christ to the world does not rest alone upon those who are ordained as *ministers* of the gospel. Each member of the church should be a living epistle, known and read of all men. A working church will be a living church. Those who are elected as *elders* and *deacons* should ever be on the alert that plans may be made and executed which will give every member of the church a share in active work for the salvation of souls. This is the only way in which the church can be preserved in a healthy, thriving condition" (*Review and Herald*, March 24, 1891, emphasis added).

102. Was Ellen White ordained by God?

> Although she was never ordained as a minister in the Seventh-day Adventist Church, Ellen White believed that God Himself had ordained her to the prophetic ministry. In her later years, while recalling her experience in the Millerite movement and receiving her first vision, she stated,

> "In the city of Portland the Lord ordained me as His messenger" (*Review and Herald*, May 18, 1911, Art. A).

> This perspective on the spiritual ordination she received from God harmonizes with her understanding that all Christians, by virtue of their baptism in Christ, are also ordained by Christ for ministry.

> "Have you tasted of the powers of the world to come? . . . Then, although ministerial hands may not have been laid upon you in ordination, Christ has laid His hands upon you and has said, 'Ye are My witnesses'" (*Testimonies for the Church*, Vol. 6, p. 444).

103. Was Ellen White given the credentials of an ordained minister?

Questions and Answers About Women's Ordination

Yes, Ellen White was given the credentials of an ordained minister. The White Estate possesses six paper credentials of an ordained minister that were given to Ellen White by the General Conference. On an 1885 certificate, the letters of the word *ordained* have been individually marked out. It is unknown when or by whom this word was "crossed out." This ought not to be interpreted to mean that church leaders thought she should not have ordained-minister credentials, as they could have issued her the credentials of an unordained minister instead, and this anomaly does not appear on her credentials issued other years. Rather, it is significant that the Adventist pioneers and Ellen White felt comfortable for her to officially hold the credentials of an ordained minister. Additionally, Ellen White was listed in editions of the *Adventist Yearbook* as an ordained minister. All existing records are consistent in categorizing her as "ordained" from 1883 to her death in 1915, though she herself declared that her ordination was of God, not of man.

104. Does Ellen White support the participation of women in pastoral ministry?

> "It is the accompaniment of the Holy Spirit of God that prepares workers, both men and women, to become pastors to the flock of God" (*Testimonies for the Church*, Vol. 6, p. 322).

> "I am wondering what can be done for the destitute fields where the flock of God is without a shepherd. . . . We need so much just now these fruits of self-denial, to support women missionaries in the field" (*Manuscript Releases*, Vol. 12, p. 164).

> "Repeatedly companies had been presented to me, reaching forth their hands in supplication, and saying, 'We are as sheep without a shepherd; come and open to us the word of God.' ... Men and women must be prepared to communicate the knowledge they have of the infinite wisdom, love, and power of God" (*General Conference Bulletin*, Apr. 1, 1899, Art. B).

Section IV: The Seventh-day Adventist Church

105. Does Ellen White support the ordination of women for the ministries to which God calls them?

In a spiritual sense, Ellen White believes all Christians have been ordained to do ministry. This perspective is at the heart of the priesthood of all believers.

"All who are ordained into the life of Christ are ordained to work for the salvation of their fellow men" (*The Signs of the Times*, Aug. 25, 1898).

In 1895, Ellen White wrote a long article about the work of laypeople in local churches. She urged ministers to let laypeople work for the church and train them to do so. And she favored that women serving in local ministry also be set apart for the kind of ministry and evangelism they do. She counseled:

> "Women who are willing to consecrate some of their time to the service of the Lord should be appointed to visit the sick, look after the young, and minister to the necessities of the poor. *They should be set apart to this work by prayer and laying on of hands.* In some cases they will need to counsel with the church officers or the minister; but if they are devoted women, maintaining a vital connection with God, they will be a power for good in the church. *This is another means of strengthening and building up the church. We need to branch out more in our methods of labor*" (*Review and Herald*, Jul. 9, 1895, emphasis added).

Here Ellen White counseled that God is leading the church in setting apart women for these various forms of ministry. It is God's will for the church to branch out, be strengthened and built up by ordaining women and men to serve in various forms of ministry and to provide care for the needs of others.

Furthermore, we should reflect carefully on the implications of some arguments of those who oppose the ordination of women. Some argue that we should not ordain women because the Bible is silent on this question. Then, what are we to make of this suggestion and counsel regarding the ordination of these women Ellen White referred to? Clearly, her understanding of both ministry and ordination are broad enough to allow for women to be

Questions and Answers About Women's Ordination

included. Ordination is both asking God's blessing on the individuals and affirming their ministry for the church.

106. Does Ellen White prescribe or prohibit the ordination of female pastors?

No. According to her secretary, C. C. Crisler (1916), Ellen White "was very careful about expressing herself ... as to the advisability of ordaining women ... [due to] the perils that such general practice would expose the church to by a gainsaying world [due to gender prejudice in the world in that era]." At the same time, Crisler writes: "This is not suggesting ... that no women are fitted for such public labor, and that none should ever be ordained" (*Daughters of God*, p. 255).

107. Did Ellen White regard the pastor as the head of the church?

Whether the pastor is a man or a woman, the pastor is never to be regarded as the head of the church. Ellen White's thought on this matter is very clear.

"God has never given a hint in His word that He has appointed any man to be the head of the church" (*The Great Controversy*, p. 51).

"Christ, not the minister, is the head of the church" (*The Signs of the Times*, Jan. 27, 1890).

"Christ is the only Head of the church" (*Manuscript Releases*, Vol. 21, p. 274).

108. Does Ellen White regard the husband as head of the family?

"How can husband and wife divide the interests of their home life and still keep a loving, firm hold upon each other? They should have a united interest in all that concerns their homemaking, and the wife, if a Christian, will have her interest

Section IV: The Seventh-day Adventist Church

with her husband as his companion; for the husband is to stand as the head of the household" (*The Adventist Home*, p. 119).

"The husband who stands as the head of his wife as Christ stands as the head of His church, who loves his wife as he loves his own body, and cherishes and nourishes her as Christ the church, will not act in a way to destroy either his own powers or the powers of his wife" (*Manuscript* 152, 1899, pp. 3, 4; *Manuscript Releases*, Vol. 4, p. 381).

"The husband is the head of the family, as Christ is the head of the church; and any course which the wife may pursue to lessen his influence and lead him to come down from that dignified, responsible position is displeasing to God. It is the duty of the wife to yield her wishes and will to her husband. Both should be yielding, but the word of God gives preference to the judgment of the husband. And it will not detract from the dignity of the wife to yield to him whom she has chosen to be her counselor, adviser, and protector. The husband should maintain his position in his family with all meekness, yet with decision" (*Testimonies for the Church*, Vol. 1, p. 307).

109. Does Ellen White regard the wife as co-head of the family?

"If the atmosphere surrounding her is the most agreeable to you, if she meets your standard for a wife to stand at the head of your family; if, in your calm judgment, taken in the light given you of God, her example would be worthy of imitation, you might as well marry her" (*Manuscript Releases*, Vol. 4, p. 217).

"Have they the knowledge that will enable them to teach others? Have they been educated to be true fathers and mothers? Can they stand at the head of a family as wise instructors? The only education worthy of the name is that which leads young

Questions and Answers About Women's Ordination

men and women to be Christlike, which fits them to bear life's responsibilities, fits them to stand at the head of their families" (*Counsels to Parents, Teachers, and Students*, p. 382).

"Every woman who is at the head of a family and yet does not understand the art of healthful cookery should determine to learn that which is so essential to the well-being of her household" (*The Ministry of Healing*, p. 303).

"Of all our training-schools, the family should stand first. Fathers and mothers should feel that they are placed at the head of a mission" (*The Signs of the Times*, May 4, 1888).

"The men and women at the head of a mission need close connection with God, in order to keep themselves pure and to know how to manage the youth discreetly, so that the thoughts of all shall be untainted, uncorrupted" (*Gospel Workers*, p. 366).

"Even though the men and women of our missions are in character as pure as fine gold, they need constant connection with God in order to keep themselves pure and to know how to manage the youth discreetly, so that all shall keep their thoughts untainted, uncorrupted" (*General Conference Daily Bulletin*, Feb. 6, 1893, Art. B).

110. Does Ellen White regard being "head" as being in a position of unilateral rulership?

"Neither husband nor wife is to make a plea for rulership. The Lord has laid down the principle that is to guide in this matter. The husband is to cherish his wife as Christ cherishes the church. And the wife is to respect and love her husband. Both are to cultivate the spirit of kindness, being determined never to grieve or injure the other. . . . Do not try to compel each other to do as you wish. You cannot do this and retain

Section IV: The Seventh-day Adventist Church

each other's love" (*The Adventist Home*, pp. 106-107).

"The Lord would have the wife render respect unto her husband, but always as it is fit in the Lord. . . . Abigail saw that . . . [h]e [Nabal] would remind her that he was the lord of his household, that she was his wife and therefore in subjection to him, and must do as he should dictate. . . . From this history, we can see that there are circumstances under which it is proper for a woman to act promptly and independently, moving with decision in the way she knows to be the way of the Lord" (*Manuscript 17*, 1891; *Manuscript Releases*, Vol. 21, pp. 213-214).

"Christ's rule is one of wisdom and love, and when husbands fulfill their obligations to their wives, they will use their authority with the same tenderness ... and in the same way that Christ requires submission from the church" (*The Adventist Home*, p. 117).

"The Lord Jesus does not rule His church like a taskmaster" (*Ibid.*). "The Lord Jesus has not been correctly represented in His relation to the church by many husbands in their relation to their wives, for they do not keep the way of the Lord. They declare that their wives must be subject to them in everything" (*Ibid.*). "But it was not the design of God that the husband should have control, as head of the house, when he himself does not submit to Christ. He must be under the rule of Christ that he may represent the relation of Christ to the church. If he is a coarse, rough, boisterous, egotistical, harsh, and overbearing man, let him never utter the word that the husband is the head of the wife, and that she must submit to him in everything; for he is not the Lord, he is not the husband in the true significance of the term" (*Ibid.*).

111. Does Ellen White recommend the use of the tithe for remuneration of female pastors?

Questions and Answers About Women's Ordination

Indirectly, yes, when she alludes to Paul's teaching on financial support for elders/pastors who labor in word and doctrine (1 Tim. 3:17-20):

"Make no mistake in neglecting to correct the error of giving ministers less than they should receive. . . . The tithe should go to those who labor in word and doctrine, be they men or women" (*Manuscript 149*, 1899, p. 3; *Manuscript Releases*, Vol. 1, p. 263).

In the 1890s, while living in Australia, Ellen White knew many spouses of ministers who worked as hard in soul-winning and evangelism as their husbands did. She believed that men and women are called by God to serve the church in gospel ministry, defined in the broadest of terms and activities. She counseled church leaders that these women should also be adequately remunerated for their work.

> "I know that the faithful women should be paid wages as it is considered proportionate to the pay received by ministers. They carry the burden of souls and should not be treated unjustly" (*Letter 137*, 1898; *Manuscript Releases*, Vol. 12, p. 161).

In fact, she considered this issue a moral issue.

> "Those who have held the fort, bearing responsibilities, are to receive just and equal remuneration. They have a love for the cause of God, and a conscientious regard for the work in all its phases, and the work needs their talents and influence. They will not leave upon the work a wrong impress. The door of temptation [i.e., to become discouraged or to give up working for the church] should not be opened to them by the inattention of their brethren. . . . Injustice must not be done to any worker" (*Manuscript 69*, 1898; *Manuscript Releases*, Vol. 12, p. 162).

It is on the basis of these thoughts that the Seventh-day Adventist Church has encouraged women to enter all aspects of ministry, to work for the church, to be remunerated fairly and equally as male co-workers, and, in some regions of the church, to be recognized equally with the same licenses and credentials.

Section IV: The Seventh-day Adventist Church

112. What does the use of the tithe for the support of women teach us about the level of participation of women in pastoral ministry?

   Some argue that when Ellen White referred to women as "pastors to the flock of God" (*Testimonies for the Church*, Vol. 6, p. 322), she was only referring to lay ministries such as canvassing. However, her support for the use of the tithe to support female ministers indicates that she did not regard these women as involved in only lay ministries. Using Paul's words (1 Tim. 5:17) that describe the work of church leaders such as elders or bishops, she states:

   > "Make no mistake in neglecting to correct the error of giving ministers less than they should receive.... The tithe should go to those who labor in word and doctrine, be they men or women" (*Manuscript Releases*, Vol. 1, p. 263).

   > "One reasons that the tithe may be applied to school purposes. Still others reason that canvassers and colporteurs should be supported from the tithe. But a great mistake is made when the tithe is drawn from the object for which it is to be used—the support of the ministers" (*Counsels on Stewardship*, p. 102).

   > "I ... will show you how I regard the tithe money being used for other purposes. This is the Lord's special revenue fund.... I have had special instruction from the Lord *that the tithe is for a special purpose, consecrated to God to sustain those who minister in the sacred work as the Lord's chosen.... There is to be special labor given to awaken the people of God who believe the truth, to give a faithful tithe to the Lord, and ministers should be encouraged and sustained by that tithe*" (*Daughters of God*, p. 256, emphasis added).

   > "The light which the Lord has given me on this subject, is that the means in the treasury for the support of the ministers in the different fields is not to be used for any other purpose. If an honest tithe were paid, and the money coming into the

Questions and Answers About Women's Ordination

treasury were carefully guarded, the ministers would receive a just wage" (*Special Testimonies for Ministers and Workers*—No. 10, p. 18).

113. Does Ellen White regard men as always better than women for church management?

No, not necessarily. In 1879, Ellen White addressed a difficult situation at the South Lancaster church in Massachusetts. She felt the ministers working in that church or in the area had not been good leaders. One pastor had "a disposition to dictate and control matters." Knowing there were "humble, devoted women" in that congregation who had been sneered at by these ministers, she made this comment:

> "It is not always men who are best adapted to the successful management of a church. If faithful women have more deep piety and true devotion than men, they could indeed by their prayers and their labors do more than men who are unconsecrated in heart and in life" (*Letter 33*, 1879; *Manuscript Releases*, Vol. 19, p. 56).

Obviously, this statement does not call for the ordination of women, but it is the beginning of a pattern in Ellen White's writings in which we see her responding to some situations by inviting the leaders of the church to consider asking women to do the work that ordained men do. This division of labor is for Ellen White conducive to facilitating the mission of the church. If more people are involved in the mission of the church, more will be accomplished.

114. Did Ellen White teach that we have already received all the light on the subject of women in ministry?

To reluctant church leaders, who did not understand the need to remunerate fairly and equally spouses who worked for the church alongside their husbands, Ellen White wrote to A. G. Daniells:

> "We need women workers to labor in connection with their husbands, and we should encourage those who wish to engage

Section IV: The Seventh-day Adventist Church

in this line of missionary effort. . . . *Study the Scriptures for further light on this point.* Women were among Christ's devoted followers in the days of His ministry, and Paul makes mention of certain women who were helpers together with him in the gospel (see Phil. 4:2-3)" (*Letter 142*, 1909; *Manuscript Releases*, Vol. 12, pp. 166-167, emphasis added).

There may be a hint of frustration in Ellen White's tone as she writes these words to a reluctant General Conference president, teaching him that since there were women disciples of Jesus and co-workers of Paul, then women should be encouraged to work for the Seventh-day Adventist Church and be treated equally and fairly for their ministry. She had a bigger vision of ministry and a more fair approach to women than did many men in leadership at the time.

115. Did Ellen White expect a progressive unfolding of God's plan for church organization?

> "The apostles must now take an important step in the perfecting of gospel order in the church by laying upon others some of the burdens thus far borne by themselves" (*The Acts of the Apostles*, pp. 88).

> "The apostles were led by the Holy Spirit to outline a plan for the better organization of all the working forces of the church" (*Ibid.*).

> "The organization of the church at Jerusalem was to serve as a model for the organization of churches in every other place. . . . [Nevertheless,] later in the history of the early church, when in various parts of the world many groups of believers had been formed into churches, the organization of the church was further perfected, so that order and harmonious action might be maintained" (*Ibid.*, pp. 90-91).

116. Did Ellen White think that women would complement men in ministry?

Questions and Answers About Women's Ordination

"When a great and decisive work is to be done, God chooses men and women to do this work, and it will feel the loss if the talents of both are not combined" (*Letter 77*, 1898; *Evangelism*, p. 469).

"In the mind of God, the ministry of men and women existed before the world was created. He determined that His ministers should have a perfect exemplification of Himself and His purposes. No human career could do this work; for God gave Christ in humanity to work out His ideal of what humanity may become. . . . Christ not only held a theory of genuine ministry, but in His humanity He wrought out an illustration of the ministry that God approves" (*Manuscript Releases*, Vol. 18, p. 380).

117. Does Ellen White teach that Eve's sin consisted of seeking to get out from under the authority of her husband?

Ellen White writes:

"She was perfectly happy in her Eden home by her husband's side; but like restless modern Eves, she was flattered that there was a higher sphere than that which God had assigned her. But in attempting to climb higher than her original position, she fell far below it" (*Testimonies for the Church*, Vol. 3, p. 483).

A careful examination of the immediate context of this statement makes clear that the "higher sphere" Eve hoped to enter was to be *like God*, not to get out from under her husband's headship. The sphere that God had assigned her was to be an equal partner "by her husband's side," not to be in submission to her husband's male domination.

Likewise, Ellen White's reference to "restless modern Eves" is not describing their attempts to usurp male headship in the home or church, but rather describes any attempt on their part to "reach positions for which He has not fitted them" (*Patriarchs and Prophets*, p. 59). This principle applies equally to men as to women, as one aspires to a position that he/she does not have the necessary

Section IV: The Seventh-day Adventist Church

preparation for filling, or abandons other work God has given him/her to do in attempts to advance in career or status.

118. Was Adam's rule over Eve part of the curse due to sin?

In *Testimonies for the Church*, Ellen White says:

> "When God created Eve, He designed that she should possess neither inferiority nor superiority to the man, but that in all things she should be his equal. . . . But after Eve's sin, as she was first in the transgression, the Lord told her that Adam should rule over her. She was to be in subjection to her husband, and this was a part of the curse" (*Testimonies for the Church*, Vol. 3, p. 484).

119. Is the curse God's ideal for male-female relationships?

The Adventist Home, p. 231, says, "Woman should fill the position which God originally designed for her, as her husband's equal."

> "Neither husband nor wife is to make a plea for rulership. The Lord has laid down the principle that is to guide in this matter. The husband is to cherish his wife as Christ cherishes the church. And the wife is to respect and love her husband. Both are to cultivate the spirit of kindness, being determined never to grieve or injure the other. . . . Do not try to compel each other to do as you wish. You cannot do this and retain each other's love" (*The Adventist Home*, pp. 106-107).

120. Did Ellen White support unity in diversity on some matters of biblical interpretation?

On the idea that we should all be thinking exactly like each other with regard to interpretations of the Bible, Ellen White said this:

> "We cannot then take a position that the unity of the church consists in viewing every text of Scripture in the very same light. The church may pass resolution upon resolution to put down all disagreement of opinions, but we cannot force the mind and will, and thus root out disagreement. These resolutions may conceal the discord, but they cannot quench it and

Questions and Answers About Women's Ordination

establish perfect agreement. Nothing can perfect unity in the church but the spirit of Christlike forbearance. Satan can sow discord; Christ alone can harmonize the disagreeing elements" (*Manuscript Releases*, Vol. 11, p. 266).

"By the power of the truth how many things might be adjusted and controversies hoary with age find quietude in the admission of better ways. The great, grand principle, 'Peace on earth and good will to men' will be far better practiced when those who believe in Christ are laborers together with God. Then all the little things which some are ever harping upon, which are not authoritatively settled by the Word of God, will not be magnified into important matters" (*Letter 183*, 1899; (*Mind, Character, and Personality*, Vol. 2, p. 499).

Ellen White herself uses the phrase "unity in diversity" many times in her writing.

"The connection of the branches with one another and with the Vine constitutes them a unity, but this does not mean uniformity in everything. Unity in diversity is a principle that pervades the whole creation" (*Review and Herald*, Nov. 9, 1897).

"The strength of God's people lies in their union with him through his only begotten Son, and their union with one another. There are no two leaves of a tree precisely alike; neither do all minds run in the same direction. But while this is so, there may be unity in diversity" (*Review and Herald*, Jul. 4, 1899, Art. A).

"It is God's plan that in his work there shall be unity in diversity. In a garden there are no two flowers just alike. Each leaf on a tree differs from every other leaf. So in the work of God, men of different minds and capabilities are needed" (*Review and Herald*, Apr. 28, 1904).

121. How does Ellen White view the headship of God—even in the act of creation?

Section IV: The Seventh-day Adventist Church

She views it as a headship of service.

> "In His life and lessons Christ has given a perfect exemplification of the unselfish ministry which has its origin in God. God does not live for Himself. By creating the world, and by upholding all things, He is constantly ministering to others. … This ideal of ministry the Father committed to His Son. Jesus was given to stand at the head of humanity, by His example to teach what it means to minister. His whole life was under a law of service. He served all, ministered to all. Again and again Jesus tried to establish this principle among His disciples. . . . He said, 'Whosoever will be great among you, let him be your minister; and whosoever will be chief among you, let him be your servant: even as the Son of man came not to be ministered unto, but to minister, and to give His life a ransom for many.' Matthew 20:26-28" (*The Acts of the Apostles*, p. 359).

Seventh-day Adventist History

122. How did the Seventh-day Adventist pioneers deal with matters where the Bible did not give explicit and detailed instructions?

   When specific topics aren't addressed in Scripture, it is considered a sound, acceptable practice to apply principles drawn from the Bible. Ellen White followed this practice in an example cited by her husband, James White, in the *Review and Herald* (April 26, 1860):

   > "If it be asked, Where are your plain texts of scripture for holding church property legally? we reply, The Bible does not furnish any; neither does it say that we should have a weekly paper, a steam printing-press, that we should publish books, build places of worship, and send out tents? Jesus says, 'Let your light so shine before men,' &c.; but he does not give all the particulars how this shall be done. The church is left to move forward in the great work, praying for divine guidance, acting upon the most efficient plans for its accomplishment. We believe it safe to be governed by the following RULE: All means which, according to sound judgment, will advance the cause of truth, are not forbidden by plain scripture declarations, should be employed."

123. How do Seventh-day Adventists understand the offices of the pastor, elder, and deacon?

   At least as far back as 1942, the official *Manual for Ministers* (pp. 11-22) noted that there were three distinct offices requiring ordination in the Adventist world church: the gospel minister, the local elder, and the deacon. In 1992, the *Seventh-day Adventist Minister's Manual* (p. 76) correctly strengthened this historic position by articulating this three-fold differentiation even more clearly, together with appropriate Scripture references. The same position is presented in the 2009 edition—now called *Seventh-day Adventist Minister's Handbook* (p. 85).

Section IV: The Seventh-day Adventist Church

124. Does the Seventh-day Adventist world church teach that since man is the head of woman, then it is wrong for women to serve as pastors, elders, or deacons?

    No. The modern headship doctrine, which teaches that Eve was created to be submissive to Adam's leadership and that women cannot hold positions of spiritual leadership in the church, was developed by a small group of Evangelical ministers in the 1980s and introduced into the Adventist denomination in 1987. Though some Adventists have vigorously advocated the male headship doctrine during the last thirty years, it has never been adopted by the Adventist world church. In fact, the Adventist denomination has officially adopted fundamental beliefs that deny the headship principle and has officially approved women serving as both elders and pastors.

125. What is the early history of Seventh-day Adventist support for women in ministry?

    The early Seventh-day Adventist denomination was remarkably progressive in its time regarding women in church leadership. Because of the ministry of Ellen White, the church had to decide very early what it believed about women doing ministry. Adventist pioneers argued vigorously from the Bible that women were not barred from public leadership in church, and the *Review and Herald* published articles to that effect: unqualified endorsements by editors James White and Uriah Smith (see Beverly G. Beem and Ginger Hanks Harwood, pp. 3, 25; *Review and Herald*, Jul. 30, 1861, pp. 65-66), plus more cautious ones by J. H. Waggoner (*The Signs of the Times*, Dec. 19, 1878, p. 380) and J. N. Andrews (*Review and Herald*, Jan. 2, 1879, p. 4).

    Although the immediate need for this research was to defend Ellen White's ministry, none of the articles were limited to her role, or to women as prophets specifically. Uriah Smith commented that, while Joel's prediction of daughters prophesying (Joel 2:28-29) "must embrace public speaking of some kind, this we think is but half of its meaning" (*Review and Herald*, Jul. 30, 1861, pp. 65-66).

126. Was there an increasing involvement of women in ministry

Questions and Answers About Women's Ordination

in the Seventh-day Adventist Church during the lifetime of Ellen White?

During Ellen White's lifetime, women were involved in various aspects of ministry. Early Adventist leaders defended the involvement of women in ministry, particularly against those who would cite the Apostle Paul's injunction that women remain silent in the church. Their arguments were based on the hermeneutical principles of comparing Scripture with Scripture, understanding the historical context of a biblical text, and examining the functions that women filled in biblical history. These principles led the early Adventist leaders in their vigorous defense of women in ministry. Ellen White also regularly added her voice to this endorsement, even urging that women be ordained who are involved in visiting the sick, looking after the young, and ministering to the necessities of the poor (*Review and Herald*, Jul. 9, 1895).

In 1868, women began to receive licenses to serve as what we would call Bible workers or evangelists. Between 1880 and 1920 there were about four to six women licentiates any given year in the denominational *Yearbook*, the greatest number being ten in 1917. Many more served in various capacities without receiving a license. Altogether, however, their numbers represented 1 to 2 percent of all licentiates. Today the percentage of women pastors in North America is still about the same.

According to editions of the *Adventist Yearbook* from 1884 (when ministerial listings first appeared) to 1915 (when Ellen White died), twenty-eight women held ministerial licenses. Of these women, only Ellen White held ordination credentials, which she received until her death. Nonetheless, the number of women functioning as pastors is noteworthy, considering the cultural context of the time. In 1881, a motion was even proposed at the General Conference to ordain qualified women as pastors. The motion was never acted upon.

127. How did the history of women in ministry unfold in the years after the death of Ellen White?

After the death of Ellen White in 1915, and with the dramatic rise of Fundamentalism in Protestant America in the 1920s and

Section IV: The Seventh-day Adventist Church

onward, the number of women serving roles of leadership plummeted. Adventist membership came to be influenced by what other conservative churches were teaching about women in leadership and ministry, who were using many of the same arguments that Uriah Smith and James White had battled against several generations before.

As Western culture shifted in the 1960s and onward, the church has reopened the question. Major studies have been commissioned over the last several decades, most of which have not been acted upon, and there has never been a consensus that there is a reason biblically, or from the writings of Ellen White, to forbid or require that women be ordained. Proposals to officially endorse the ordination of women at the General Conference level, or to give the North American Division special permission to do so, have been declined because of the lack of worldwide acceptance of the practice.

Nonetheless, the number of women in ministry has steadily increased in North America and in many parts of the world church. Women have pursued theological and ministerial degrees at our educational institutions for many decades, and women now serve as local pastors and at all levels of church leadership.

128. How and why did the Adventist Church begin credentialing and ordaining ministers?

In the earliest years, the Adventist Church had ministers who had been ordained in their previous denominations, and it resisted creating church authority structures that would make it like other churches. However, as the movement grew, there were practical problems with being able to know who was a legitimate Sabbatarian preacher and who was not. James White argued for giving credentials to ministers to clear up the problem:

> "How then can it be right for our preachers to enter new fields to meet wily opponents without papers showing their church relation and standing? The cause of truth has sometimes suffered for want of such papers. We say, Let every preacher have them, and let them be renewed every year. This course would open the way for our preachers, and would save

Questions and Answers About Women's Ordination

our brethren from the abuse of imposters" (*Review and Herald*, Aug. 27, 1861).

Of course, the time came when the church needed to ordain ministers who had not been ordained by another denomination. Since most preachers began as volunteers, not employees, church leadership could watch their ministry for a time before deciding to ordain and credential them.

129. Why are some ministers ordained, and others not? Why aren't all ministers ordained at hiring?

In the early years of the church, the practice was to watch new ministers for a time to see that God was truly working through them. As church leaders saw the minister's work bearing fruit, the ordination service was a confirmation, or recognition, of God's call. This was quite reasonable, as most began as volunteers. And furthermore, in the early years of our church, only pastors serving as evangelists were ordained; others were not. The practice of delaying ordination is continued today, even though most pastors begin their careers as hired employees. This is why ministers are not ordained immediately upon being hired. The purpose was not to create two levels of ministry, or two classes of pastors—although it ended up doing exactly this—but in order that ordination could be the church recognizing a gift that had already been demonstrated.

Additionally, to circumvent the fact that a newly hired pastor is not ordained, the conference requests that the young minister be ordained as a local church elder, thus providing the new pastor with an ordained-elder credential. It is in this capacity that a new pastor functions until ministerial ordination is conferred. The later ordination as a minister adds very little to what the pastor can do for the church and serves primarily as a confirmation and recognition of God's call. Thus our practice of ministerial ordination is better described as a commissioning, since the ordination to be authorized to do ministry (preaching; leading the church; baptizing; officiating at Lord's Supper, weddings, and funerals, etc.) occurs at the elder's level.

130. What practical differences are there between an ordained

Section IV: The Seventh-day Adventist Church

and an unordained minister?

In light of previous actions of the General Conference, from a policy perspective there is little difference. Only an ordained minister is authorized to be a conference president, organize churches, and conduct the service of ordination for other ministers. However, ordination is very important because it provides the endorsement of the organized church as it recognizes a person's spiritual gifts.

131. What is the current church policy on gender and ordination?

The *General Conference Working Policy* on ordination does not mention requirements for gender. Neither is there a gender requirement for ordination included elsewhere in the policy. The ordination segment uses male language, instead of being gender inclusive, and the policy regarding discrimination in employment makes an exception allowing gender discrimination for jobs requiring ordination (though it does not require such discrimination). Neither of these factors constitutes a policy forbidding the ordination of a woman.

132. Why does the church hire women as ministers but not ordain them?

Women are hired as pastors because church leaders see their gifts and recognize their calling. The idea that a conference hires a woman to serve as pastor, assigns her to pastor a particular congregation, and pays her but does not recognize her as called and gifted by God, makes no sense at all. However, because there has not been a consensus in the church on what the Bible teaches about the ordination of women, the decision to not go forward was more pragmatic than biblical. The delay has also been influenced by the fact that in some places it would be regarded as highly unusual and possibly scandalous to recognize a woman with ordination.

This compromise, however, is not biblically consistent. As ordination is an act of recognition and confirmation, and it bestows no authority beyond the authority to do the job one is called to (see the example of Acts 13:1-3), there is no reason to withhold it.

Questions and Answers About Women's Ordination

If one is called and capable of serving a ministry, there is no biblical reason not to acknowledge it by the act of laying on of hands. The dividing line at the point of ordination comes from a wrong view of ordination, a medieval view that made ordination a "sacrament," which confers special virtue on the person ordained.

133. Has the Seventh-day Adventist Church repeatedly voted that it would be unbiblical to ordain women?

No. In the 1990 vote, the explanation includes "the commission does not have a consensus as to whether or not the Scriptures and the writings of EGW explicitly advocate or deny the ordination of women to pastoral ministry." Essentially this was a pragmatic decision, not a biblical decision. In 1995, the church did not take an official position on the biblical support (or lack of it) for the ordination of women to the ministry. It simply voted against leaving the decision up to each world division "at this time."

While some people say the decisions to not approve ordinations of women at the 1990 and 1995 General Conference Sessions function as some kind of "quasi-policy," neither action was presented as policy, voted as policy, or added to the official *General Conference Working Policy* book.

The church had no gender-specific ordination requirements before 1990 and 1995 General Conference Sessions and none after.

134. What is the Seventh-day Adventist position on men and women as elders?

"Elders and deacons should be persons of experience, chosen wisely. By action of the Annual Council of 1975, reaffirmed at the 1984 Annual Council, both men and women are eligible to serve as elders and receive ordination to this position of service in the church" (*Seventh-day Adventist Minister's Handbook*, 2009, p. 94).

135. What is the official position of the Seventh-day Adventist Church on women as pastors?

On October 5, 1989, the General Conference Committee voted to refer to the 1990 General Conference Session a recommendation

Section IV: The Seventh-day Adventist Church

that (1) women not be ordained, but that (2) commissioned women pastors "may perform essentially the ministerial functions of an ordained minister." But on October 9, 1989, the same committee voted to split that action, sending the recommendation that women not be ordained to the 1990 General Conference Session, but immediately authorizing commissioned women pastors to perform essentially the ministerial functions of an ordained minister. (General Conference Committee Minutes, October 5, 1989, 89-384-389, and October 9, 1989, 89-429-431.)

136. Has the church initiated new patterns and precedents for details of church life without explicit biblical instruction concerning these specific policies?

Yes. Some examples include specific times for the start of Sabbath School and the divine worship hour, Communion services once per quarter, building churches instead of meeting in homes, avoiding the use of the term *bishop* to identify pastors and elders, publishing Sabbath School lesson guides, establishing Pathfinders, and building and operating sanitariums and hospitals.

Current Discussion

137. What were the general perspectives that developed in various groups within the Theology of Ordination Study Committee?

Because answers to questions regarding ordination, and specifically women's ordination, must be sought from biblical principles and are not always clearly taught in the Scriptures, there were a variety of opinions among the members of the committee at the outset. In the end, however, it became evident that the views of the committee members coalesced into three predominant perspectives.

The first group believed that ordination of women to either local or global ministry as pastors or elders goes against the teachings of the Bible and that even an elder, who holds a position of headship in the church, must be male. For this group, male headship is a rule in the home and in the church.

The second, numerically largest, group of participants believed that ministry in the church is related to spiritual gifting and that there is nothing in the Scriptures that should prevent women from receiving the spiritual blessing given to them through the rite of ordination. This group affirmed that headship in the church belongs to Jesus alone, thus underlining the impossibility of either male or female headship in the church. Those belonging to this group also affirmed that women's ordination should proceed only in those areas where it is acceptable to the majority of church members.

Finally, during the last meeting of the Theology of Ordination Study Committee, it became evident that a third view had emerged. Those accepting the third perspective believed that while male leadership under the headship of Christ appears to be the biblical ideal, it would be appropriate for regional denominational leadership to make the decision whether to ordain women to the gospel ministry in their area.

138. What are the general perspectives indicated in the reports from the various divisions of the General Conference?

Section IV: The Seventh-day Adventist Church

Each of the thirteen divisions of the worldwide Seventh-day Adventist Church presented a report reflective of the diverse set of countries and cultures that compose its geographical area. In spite of the variance of viewpoints, there was an overarching commonality in understanding that though ordination is a function of the church, only God can call and anoint His servants. In regard to the question of the gender of the one ordained, the majority of the divisions expressed a desire to accept a variety of practices, for the sake of the gospel moving forward around the world. It was recognized by many that a conservative, biblically grounded conviction is held by people for and against ordaining women to pastoral ministry. In light of this conflicting biblical conviction, most divisions agreed that (1) the church must make room for a variance of practice around the world, and (2) no division must be forced to act in a way that does not fit its mission territory.

The Way Forward

139. Isn't church unity jeopardized if only some parts of the world ordain women?

Throughout Adventist history we have often faced theological and ecclesiastical issues that have caused differences among us. Despite vigorous debate at times, we have remained united as one body under Christ pursuing our unique God-given mission.

> "We cannot then take a position that the unity of the church consists in viewing every text of Scripture in the very same light. . . . Nothing can perfect unity in the church but the spirit of Christlike forbearance" (Ellen G. White, "Love, the Need of the Church," *Manuscript Releases*, Vol. 11, p. 266).

Fundamental Belief No. 14 on "Unity in the Body of Christ" states:

> "Distinctions of race, culture, learning, nationality, and differences between high and low, rich and poor, male and female, must not be divisive among us. We are all equal in Christ, who by one Spirit has bonded us into one fellowship with Him and with one another. We are to serve and be served without partiality or reservation."

On the basis of this Fundamental Belief, the General Conference has established policies regulating responsibilities within the church, including employment practices recognizing women in leadership roles (see GC Working Policy BA-60). These policies reflect our convictions on the doctrine of spiritual gifts: that the Holy Spirit calls both men and women to service and that all spiritual gifts are gender inclusive (1 Cor. 12:11; Joel 2:28-29; Acts 2:17-21). The church has taken action to allow for the ordination of deaconesses and female elders and the commissioning of female pastors.

Although these church policies and practices are implemented differently throughout the world, the church has remained a unified, worldwide organization pressing together in mission and message. Each area would choose what best promotes the mission

Section IV: The Seventh-day Adventist Church

of the church in their field. No entity would be coerced, no union forced to act outside of its collective constituents' conviction.

140. Is church unity best served by identical or varying practices with regard to the ordination of women?

There are ordained ministers in our church today who would not be effective everywhere in the world because of language and culture. Suitability is a paramount factor when a minister is appointed to a position. Acceptance of diversity in the various divisions brings unity, not disunity.

In recent decades, the General Conference has approved policies recognizing women in leadership roles: the ordination of deaconesses and elders and the commissioning of pastors. Although these policies are not practiced in all regions of the world, the church has remained a single, worldwide organization.

141. Why is the issue of the ordination of women as elders or pastors of such crucial importance for the Seventh-day Adventist Church at this time?

Paul wrote Galatians 3:27-28 in the first century. It took two more centuries before the Christian church ceased discriminating against Greeks and nineteen centuries before the Christian church advocated for the abolition of slavery. Perhaps the time is ripe for Adventist Christians to break down the walls of gender discrimination and acknowledge that the Holy Spirit anoints whom He will, for the task to which He calls. Ellen White wrote:

> "In every age there is a new development of truth, a message of God to the people of that generation" (*Christ's Object Lessons*, p. 127).

142. In an issue such as gender roles, which is so culturally influenced, how much should the church be responsive to the culture in which it ministers?

There needs to be a balance. We are to be sensitive, but the message of the gospel should not be compromised by culture. There are clashes. For instance, we do not accept "cultural rape." The United States has a culture of cinema violence, materialism,

Questions and Answers About Women's Ordination

unbiblical sexuality, and profanity, but our Adventist message contradicts these aspects of U.S. culture.

At the same time, in some circumstances of strong and ingrained societal gender prejudice, it may be necessary to allow less than God's ideal for the sake of bringing the Advent message to all the people.

Though slavery is morally wrong and though the Christian church over time became a major force in eradicating it from the Roman Empire, God did not put that issue first on the agenda for the apostles. So, at times we will have to let the core of the gospel do its work, not expecting a group of people to learn in one generation what it has taken the people of God generations to understand.

143. How do we balance the biblical principle involved in the call of some women to specific ministry roles with the biblical principle that we should not offend others who see this as biblically wrong?

We answer by quoting the Swiss Reformer Huldrych Zwingli who, of course in a different context, expressed that "whoever through ... ignorance wants to take offense without cause should not be permitted to remain in his ... ignorance but should be strengthened in order that he may not regard as sinful what is not sinful" (Cochrane, p. 41-42).

Showing that women's ordination is in full accordance with biblical principles and God's ideal is the primary reason for this book!

144. What advice would you give to a young woman who feels called to full-time ministry?

Become a minister of Christ. Don't push or insist, but preach the gospel and present the Advent message whenever you have opportunity. Serve as a human being called by God to proclaim His truth, not because you are a woman. Serve because you have been anointed by the Holy Spirit and called by Jesus Christ to represent Him, not yourself or a gender agenda.

The corporate church today provides such opportunities. Policies are in place so female ministers may share many responsibilities, and though you will definitely encounter your share of human

Section IV: The Seventh-day Adventist Church

opposition, there are rich and wonderful rewards and blessings in following your call.

The corporate church needs such role models to persuade the skeptics and inspire other women to serve. Many of our church members are kind and gentle Christians who will be grateful for your contributions.

145. What advice would you give to a member of a congregation to whom having a woman pastor just seems wrong?

The Adventist community worldwide exceeds twenty million people. For most of us, there will, of course, be elements of the life, practice, or teachings of the church with which we agree more or less. When we agree "less," our disagreements are to be expressed with Christian kindness and courtesy. Additionally, it is important that we make an attempt to question our own presuppositions to determine whether they are really driven by Scripture or driven by our culture, experience, or "favorite preacher."

It is important to consider the views of the pioneers of the Seventh-day Adventist Church. In contrast with the prevailing Christian American culture of the time, they argued strongly for female preachers of the gospel in a series of articles in the *Review and Herald* during the 1850s.

Learn also from the position of our pioneers regarding female preachers and from the decisions of the corporate church. The Seventh-day Adventist Church has voted to accept female preachers and elders, and commissioned female ministers are fully qualified to perform baptisms, marriages, and other church functions. The position of the church on these issues is clear.

But more than that, the authority is the Word of God, never the preacher—whether male or female. We do not, for instance, as in some charismatic circles, submit to the authority of any leader because of his or her charismatic gifts and supposed direct link to God, independent of the Word. The Bible is the source of our doctrinal authority, not the role of any leader. Creating or accepting such an "authoritative" teaching role in the church will set aside the Bible.

This does not imply that pastors do not have an authority to teach that comes from Christ and His inspired Word. Furthermore,

Questions and Answers About Women's Ordination

our leaders are appointed or elected by the church and in relation to the organization receive their authority from the church. They may be replaced, and they are replaced from time to time. The role of our leaders is not to decide the message, but rather themselves to submit to the message and to the church at large. And as we elect them, we should respect their right to exercise the authority we give them in the appropriate areas.

Let us illustrate this point by referring to one of the most exciting events during the awakenings in the 1840s. In Sweden at that time, laypersons were not allowed to preach or even to gather people in homes for Bible studies. To create revival, God called children, between the ages of six and ten, to preach the Word. They would read from the Bible in public places and in gatherings in homes with a clear voice, calling for conversion and commitment to Jesus, appealing for a sober life and preparation for the second coming of Jesus. Though many of these children were incarcerated and tortured, they continued their biblical preaching, led by the Holy Spirit.

If a girl at the age of six preaches truthfully from the Bible, the authority of that message stands above the authority of any elder or ordained minister who preaches contrary to the Word of God. This, according to Matthew 7:20, is the measure by which we judge anyone who ministers or leads—regardless of gender.

146. **It seems that many denominations that ordain women also ordain practicing homosexuals. Why should we follow their lead?**

The Adventist Church doesn't seek to pattern itself after others. Rather, we have studied Scripture and examined numerous resources leading to our recommendations. Although the Theology of Ordination Study Committee members have researched this topic intensely over a two-year time span, questions about ordination have been under examination since 1881, when a resolution recommending the ordination of women to ministry was presented at the General Conference Session.

The Adventist denomination has consistently had a vision for elevating the human race by returning to the model found in the Garden of Eden. Two illustrations of this are Sabbath-keeping and

Section IV: The Seventh-day Adventist Church

vegetarianism. Uplifting the theology of the Eden model, along with the direct biblical references condemning homosexual behavior in the Old and New Testaments, prevents our church from ordination of those engaged in homosexual behavior. However, the Bible does not prescribe or prohibit the ordination of women, and it consistently elevates women above the cultural norms of the fallen world.

147. Is ordaining women the response of our church to the feminist movement, and would it then be a form of following the world?

The ordination of women was first formally proposed in the Adventist world church back in 1881, when a resolution was presented by the Resolutions Committee at the General Conference Session. (That resolution was forwarded to the General Conference Executive Committee, and no action was taken.) In the last fifty years, women's ordination has been formally researched and debated within Adventism. The recommendations of Group 2 in the Theology of Ordination Study Committee, as well as the NAD Theology of Ordination Study Committee, are the result of prayerful study of Scripture and history, theory and practice, not an attempt to comply with the standard of the world.

148. Do women and men have fundamentally different but equal roles?

It is evident in both the Bible and the modern church that every individual has been given different gifts by God. Not all male pastors play the same roles in the churches they serve. Some are gifted in public evangelism, some in prayer and spiritual nurture, some in teaching, some in starting new churches, etc. That variety of gifts is widened when women pastors serve beside men. The Seventh-day Adventist Church has never taken the position, nor found in Scripture, that God has limited the roles to which He may call and equip any faithful servant, whether young or old, male or female.

149. Isn't it a sin to seek power and authority? Why do women want to be ordained?

Questions and Answers About Women's Ordination

Men and women who are carrying out the commission given them by God in gospel ministry appreciate the recognition by the church that the Holy Spirit has gifted them for their task. Neither men nor women should seek ordination for power or authority.

The movement to ordain qualified women to ministry is not the result of women wanting to be ordained. It is the result of men and women wishing to give full expression to the gospel of Jesus Christ, which is available to all God's children, and it is the result of men and women wishing to fully recognize and utilize all the gifts that God gives to the church for the finishing of His work. In many parts of the world, failure to recognize women as equally called by God hinders the mission of the church—both in reaching the lost and in retaining our own youth.

150. How much is recognizing and affording equality of opportunity, of giftedness, of ministry, a biblical imperative for the church? How much is it a cultural discussion?

Justice is a biblical principle. Equal pay for equal work and responsibility is in accordance with biblical ethics. At the same time, we must acknowledge that opportunities within the church will be impacted by the opportunities within the specific culture where a church operates.

A number of the functions of the church are directly related to its public relations. In some cultures, for example, young people might have relatively better opportunities than in other cultures to serve the church in some functions. The same is true for different genders, not because of different values in the eyes of God as such, but because of the need of the church to function most efficiently in its particular culture, enhancing the chances of proclaiming and sharing the gospel.

151. With regard to policy, what might be a way forward for our church with regard to the ordination of female pastors?

Biblical education and cultural sensitivity must go hand in hand. As a prophetic movement, we need a clearer understanding of the nature of the Protestant message regarding the authority structure of the papacy, which in reality is the foundation for most theological objections against female participation in pastoral ministry.

Section IV: The Seventh-day Adventist Church

Further, we need to develop cultural self-awareness, realizing more fully the biases of our own culture so as not to impose them on either biblical texts or other people.

Group 2 from the Theology of Ordination Study Committee has proposed a way forward[1] that we would like to invite you to prayerfully consider:

> "Throughout Adventist history we have often faced theological and ecclesiastical issues that have caused differences among us. Despite vigorous debate at times, we have remained united as one body under Christ pursuing our unique God-given mission. 'We cannot then take a position that the unity of the church consists in viewing every text of Scripture in the very same light. . . . Nothing can perfect unity in the church but the spirit of Christlike forbearance' (Ellen G. White, 'Love, the Need of the Church,' *Manuscript Releases*, Vol. 11, p. 266).
>
> "Fundamental Belief No. 14 on 'Unity in the Body of Christ' states that 'Distinctions of race, culture, learning, nationality, and differences between high and low, rich and poor, male and female, must not be divisive among us. We are all equal in Christ, who by one Spirit has bonded us into one fellowship with Him and with one another. We are to serve and be served without partiality or reservation.' On the basis of this Fundamental Belief, the General Conference has established policies regulating responsibilities within the Church including employment practices recognizing women in leadership roles (see GC Working Policy BA-60). These policies reflect our convictions on the doctrine of spiritual gifts: that the Holy Spirit calls both men and women to service and that all spiritual gifts are gender inclusive (1 Cor. 12:11; Joel 2:28, 29; Acts 2:17-21). The Church has taken action to allow for the ordination of deaconesses and female elders and the commissioning of female pastors. Although these church policies and practices are implemented differently throughout the world, the church has remained a unified, worldwide organization pressing together in mission and message.
>
> "Following the Bible and the counsel of Ellen White, the Church acknowledges the need to adapt its practices to the

Questions and Answers About Women's Ordination

needs of the people it seeks to reach. Regional diversity in the practice of women's ordination will ensure that no entity will be compelled to do so against the will of its constituency. As in other matters, faithfulness to Scripture and mutual respect for one another are essential for the unity of the Church.

"Therefore, because we accept the Bible's call to give witness to God's impartiality and believe that disunity and fragmentation will be the inevitable result of enforcing only one perspective in all regions, we propose that:

- "Each entity responsible for calling pastors be authorized to choose either to have only men as ordained pastors or to have both men and women as ordained pastors. [This choice will be protected by guarantees in the relevant documents of each union, division, and the General Conference, so that no entity can be directed against its will to adopt a position other than the one to which the collective conscience of its constituency points.]

- "The union, at which organizational level decisions for ordination have historically been made in the Seventh-day Adventist Church, is to be enabled by its division to make the decision as to whether to approve the ordination of both men and women to gospel ministry.

"We hereby rededicate our lives to God and allegiance to His Word as we fulfil the Great Commission the Lord has entrusted to His Church. *Maranatha.* Come, Lord Jesus."

---

1. The remainder of this answer is reprinted from the Way Forward Statement 2 produced by Group 2 at the June 2014 meeting of the Theology of Ordination Study Committee. Available online at http://www.adventistarchives.org/way-forward-statement-2.pdf.

Works Cited

Andrews, J. N., "May Women Speak in Meeting?" *Review and Herald*, Jan. 2, 1879, p. 4.

Beem, Beverly G., and Ginger Hanks Harwood, "'Your Daughters Shall Prophesy': James White, Uriah Smith, and the 'Triumphant Vindication of the Right of the Sisters' to Preach" (paper presented at the annual conference of Association of Adventist Women, St. Louis, MO, 2005). Available online at http://session.adventistfaith.org/assets/393508.

General Conference Committee Minutes, October 5, 1989, 89-384-389, and October 9, 1989, 89-429-431. Available online at http://www.adventistarchives.org/gc-executive-committee-extracts-on-ordination.pdf.

General Conference Working Policy BA-60.

Manual for Ministers (Takoma Park, MD: General Conference of Seventh-day Adventists, 1942).

"Methods of Bible Study: Presuppositions, Principles, and Methods" (Silver Spring, MD: General Conference of Seventh-day Adventists, 1986). Online at http://www.adventist.org/information/official-statements/documents/article/go/0/methods-of-bible-study/12/.

Seventh-day Adventist Minister's Handbook (Silver Spring, MD: General Conference Ministerial Association, 2009).

Seventh-day Adventist Minister's Manual (Silver Spring, MD: Ministerial Association, General Conference of Seventh-day Adventists, 1992).

Waggoner, J. H., "Woman's Place in the Gospel," *The Signs of the Times*, Dec. 19, 1878, p. 380.

White, Ellen G., *The Acts of the Apostles* (Mountain View, CA: Pacific Press, 1911).

White, Ellen G., *The Adventist Home* (Washington, DC: Review and Herald, 1952).

White, Ellen G., *Christ's Object Lessons* (Washington, DC: Review and Herald, 1900).

White, Ellen G., *Counsels on Stewardship* (Washington, DC: Review and Herald, 1940).

Questions and Answers About Women's Ordination

White, Ellen G., *Counsels to Parents, Teachers, and Students* (Mountain View, CA: Pacific Press, 1913).

White, Ellen G., *Daughters of God* (Hagerstown, MD: Review and Herald, 1998).

White, Ellen G., *The Desire of Ages* (Mountain View, CA: Pacific Press, 1898).

White, Ellen G., *Evangelism* (Washington, DC: Review and Herald, 1946).

White, Ellen G., *General Conference Bulletin*, Feb. 6, 1893, Art. B; Apr. 1, 1899, Art. B.

White, Ellen G., *Gospel Workers* (Washington, DC: Review and Herald, 1915).

White, Ellen G., *The Great Controversy Between Christ and Satan* (Mountain View, CA: Pacific Press, 1911).

White, Ellen G., *Mind, Character, and Personality*, Vol. 2 (Nashville, TN: Southern Publishing, 1977).

White, Ellen G., *Manuscript Releases*, Vol. 1 (Silver Spring, MD: Ellen G. White Estate, 1981).

White, Ellen G., *Manuscript Releases*, Vol. 4 (Silver Spring, MD: Ellen G. White Estate, 1990).

White, Ellen G., *Manuscript Releases*, Vol. 11 (Silver Spring, MD: Ellen G. White Estate, 1990).

White, Ellen G., *Manuscript Releases*, Vol. 12 (Silver Spring, MD: Ellen G. White Estate, 1990).

White, Ellen G., *Manuscript Releases*, Vol. 18 (Silver Spring, MD: Ellen G. White Estate, 1990).

White, Ellen G., *Manuscript Releases*, Vol. 19 (Silver Spring, MD: Ellen G. White Estate, 1990).

White, Ellen G., *Manuscript Releases*, Vol. 21 (Silver Spring, MD: Ellen G. White Estate, 1993).

White, Ellen G., *The Ministry of Healing* (Mountain View, CA: Pacific Press, 1905).

White, Ellen G., *Our Father Cares* (Hagerstown, MD: Review and Herald, 1991).

White, Ellen G., *Patriarchs and Prophets* (Washington, DC: Review and Herald, 1890).

White, Ellen G., *Review and Herald*, Jul. 9, 1895.

White, Ellen G., *Review and Herald*, Nov. 9, 1897.

Works Cited

White, Ellen G., *Review and Herald*, Jul. 4, 1899, Art. A.

White, Ellen G., *Review and Herald*, Apr. 28, 1904.

White, Ellen G., *Review and Herald*, June 15, 1905.

White, Ellen G., "An Appeal to Our Churches Throughout the United States," *Review and Herald*, May 18, 1911, Art. A.

White, Ellen G., *The Signs of the Times*, May 4, 1888; Jan. 27, 1890; Aug. 25, 1898.

White, Ellen G., *Special Testimonies for Ministers and Workers*—No. 10 (1897).

White, Ellen G., *Testimonies for the Church*, Vol. 1 (Mountain View, CA: Pacific Press, 1868).

White, Ellen G., *Testimonies for the Church*, Vol. 3 (Mountain View, CA: Pacific Press, 1875).

White, Ellen G., *Testimonies for the Church*, Vol. 6 (Mountain View, CA: Pacific Press, 1901).

White, James, *Review and Herald*, Apr. 26, 1860.

White, James, *Review and Herald*, Aug. 27, 1861.

"Women as Preachers and Lecturers," James White and Uriah Smith, Eds., *Review and Herald*, Jul. 30, 1861, Vol. 18, No. 9. Available online at http://egwtext.whiteestate.org/publication.php?pubtype=Book&bookCode=EGWVRWSDA&lang=en&collection=6&section=all&pagenumber=13&paragraphReferences=1.

"Zwingli's Sixty-Seven Articles (of Faith) of 1523, # XLVIII," in *Reformed Confessions of the Sixteenth Century,* Arthur C. Cochrane, Ed. (Louisville, KY: Westminster John Knox Press, 2003), pp. 41-42.

Appendix A

On the Unique Headship of Christ in the Church: A Statement of the Seventh-day Adventist Theological Seminary

Preamble

We, the faculty of the Seventh-day Adventist Theological Seminary, affirm that Christ is the only head of the church (Eph. 1:22; 5:23; Col. 1:18). Therefore, while there exists legitimate leadership in the church, no other human being may rightfully claim a headship role in the church. As head of the church, Christ provides the ultimate manifestation of God's love (Eph. 5:23, 25), demonstrating and vindicating God's moral government of love (Rom. 3:4, 25-26 5:8), and thus defeating the counterfeit government of the usurping "ruler of this world" (John 12:31; 16:11).[1]

God's Moral Government of Love

Christ's headship in the church is inextricably bound up with the love of God and is itself the ultimate explication of God's love for the world (John 3:16; 15:13; Rom. 5:8). As the sole "head of the church," Christ "loved the church and gave himself up for her" (Eph. 5:23, 25).[2] Christ's demonstration of divine love as head of the church directly reflects God's moral government of love, within which the law is a transcript of God's character and, conversely, love is itself the fulfillment of God's law (Matt. 22:37-39; Rom. 13:8).[3]

Since love requires moral freedom, God does not exercise His headship power or authority to coerce or determine the moral will of His created beings. God permitted rebellion, at the highest cost to Himself, because He desires willing obedience that is motivated by love rather than fear. Such voluntary obedience could not be obtained by the exercise of power or authority, but can only be freely given. In this way, God's government is based on freely bestowed mutual love wherein God does not deterministically impose His will, but does hold intelligent creatures morally accountable to His perfect law of love.

Accordingly, rather than exercising His infinite power to unilaterally prevent or overturn the rebellion by removing the freedom necessary for a genuine love relationship, God has allowed the enemy's counterfeit government to manifest itself, while actively demonstrating the nature of His moral government of love in direct and striking contrast. Whereas the enemy grasps for power and domination, Christ, who possesses all power, does not dominate, determine, or coerce but "made Himself of no reputation, taking the form of a bondservant [*doulos*] . . . He humbled Himself and became obedient to the point of death, even the death of the cross" (Phil. 2:7-9, NKJV). In this way, Christ, the unique head of the church, "demonstrates His own love toward us, in that while we were yet sinners, Christ died for us" (Rom. 5:8). Consequently, God's government of unselfish love is clearly and supremely manifested.

The Great Controversy Between Christ and Satan

The Great Controversy originated with Satan's direct attack against the nature and role of Christ in heaven, seeking to displace Christ and exalt himself to be like God (Isa. 14:12-14; Ezek. 28:12-19; cf. Rev. 12:7-9). In the history of the Great Controversy, the usurping "ruler of this world" (John 12:31; 14:30; 16:11; cf. 2 Cor. 4:4), although defeated at the cross, continues his quest to exalt himself by dominating others. He attempts to replace God's government of love with an alternative form of government that grasps for a domineering, self-seeking authority. He seeks to replace Christ as the head (2 Thess. 2:3-4),

Appendix A

injuring both Christ, the sole head of the true church, and Christ's corporate body, His church.

From the second century onward, post-Apostolic Christianity gradually implemented a system of church government that reflected Rome's conception of authority as the power to arbitrarily command and coerce obedience and replaced the headship of Christ with the headship of mere humans. This counterfeit system of church governance was (1) hierarchical, based on a chain of command with a monarchical bishop at the "head" of the church, with complete and final control over its affairs; (2) sacramental, meaning that the spiritual life of believers, including their very salvation, depended on ordained clergymen; (3) elitist (i.e., sacerdotal), meaning that the rite of ordination (laying on of hands) infused the clergy with special powers; and (4) headship-oriented, meaning that those who received the rite of ordination were thereby married to their church and thus took on "headship" roles in the church in place of Christ the Head ("*in persona Christi Capitis*"; cf. *Vicarius Filii Dei*, "in the place of the Son of God").

This system of government has been implemented in various forms, amounting to the usurpation of Christ's headship in the church by mere humans. Indeed, this very system is that of the sea beast of Revelation 13-14, which was granted power and authority by the dragon (13:2, 4), counterfeits the resurrection of Christ (13:3), accepts the world's worship along with the dragon (13:4, 8), blasphemes against God and His sanctuary, and exercises worldwide authority to persecute God's people (13:5-7). This antichrist power, which usurps the role of Christ on earth in keeping with the ancient attempt by Satan to replace Christ in heaven, seeks to destroy the everlasting gospel and ultimately commands obedience and enforces false worship. This culminates in severe persecution of those who refuse to worship the beast and his image, the remnant who keep the commandments of God and have the faith of Jesus, those who place no confidence in mere humans with regard to their salvation (Rev. 13:6-8; 14:6-12).

The antichrist system of church government sets the stage for the

Questions and Answers About Women's Ordination

climactic events of the final conflict in Revelation by, among other things: (1) asserting authority to appoint humans to Christ-replacing headship positions in the church on earth (globally and locally), thereby (2) claiming to uniquely possess authority to interpret and teach Scripture and thus have the final word on all matters of doctrine and ecclesial practice, while (3) wielding the spiritual power and authority to command and coerce obedience using both spiritual and civil tools.

This system of government stands in direct contrast to Christ's headship and His teaching on the nature of the authority of church leaders. Christ reflected God's moral government of love by exemplifying service leadership (Matt. 20:28; Mark 10:45), including a kind of authority that does not seek to subject the wills of others or enforce obedience. Rather, it leads by the example of service and unselfish love, which draws (rather than compels) others to willing service in love (Gal. 5:13). All authority "in heaven and on earth" was given to Christ (Matt. 28:18), but Christ does not remove graciously endowed free will and force His created human beings into obedience, but "loved [us] and gave Himself up for us" (Eph. 5:2). The closest the church comes to acts of enforcement is when it engages in discipline as a corporate body, based on very clear teachings of Scripture. Such discipline is not the responsibility of any one person, or even a small group, but must be an action of at least the local congregation. Even then, such discipline does not result in coercion, but in restricting the individual from privileges of membership for a time in order to allow them to come to repentance and restoration (Matt. 18:12-17; 1 Cor. 5:5).

Church members (including but not limited to church leaders) are called to follow Christ's example of unselfish love (Eph. 5:1). They are to have the mind of Christ, which includes the willingness to humble oneself and take on the role of a slave [*doulos*] (Phil. 2:5-8) or servant [*diakonos*] of Christ (Matt. 20:26), even as He humbled Himself to the point of death. Whereas the leaders in the Roman Empire of Christ's time "lord it over them, and their great men exercise authority over

Appendix A

them" (Matt. 20:25), it is not to be so with God's people but "whoever wishes to become great among you shall be your servant [*diakonos*], and whoever wishes to be first among you shall be your slave [*doulos*]" (Matt. 20:26-27).

"For even the Son of Man did not come to be served, but to serve, and to give His life a ransom for many" (Mark 10:45). Thus, the one who would be great is the one who is the slave [*doulos*] of all (Mark 10:44), and the "greatest among you shall be your servant [*diakonos*]" (Matt. 23:11; cf. 9-12). The Bible outlines essential roles of leadership and authority in the church. However, all leadership within the church must be servant leadership. The apostle Peter adroitly balances the affirmation of leadership within the church with the humility that such leadership entails: "Therefore, I exhort the elders among you, as *your* fellow elder and witness of the sufferings of Christ . . . shepherd the flock of God among you, exercising oversight not under compulsion, but voluntarily, according to *the will of* God; and not for sordid gain, but with eagerness; nor yet as lording it over those allotted to your charge, but proving to be examples to the flock. . . . You younger men, likewise, be subject to *your* elders; and all of you, clothe yourselves with humility toward one another, for God is opposed to the proud, but gives grace to the humble. Therefore humble yourselves under the mighty hand of God, that He may exalt you at the proper time" (1 Pet. 5:1-3, 5-7).[4] Accordingly, church leaders should be humble servants. At the same time they should be respected and deeply appreciated for their diligent labor (1 Thess. 5:12; 1 Tim. 5:17; cf. Heb. 13:7) even as they also show proper respect to others by demonstrating the mutual love and regard for others that is to take place among all Christians (1 Pet. 2:17).[5]

The authority of those leading the church is conveyed to them by the church. This authority is delegated by Christ to His church and implemented through its representative system. Thus appointed leaders become stewards of a power that should be exercised on behalf of Christ and for the benefit of those they lead. The functionality of

Questions and Answers About Women's Ordination

authority does not negate equality among the members given to the church by Christ. As the Spirit leads the body of Christ, not just the few in leadership, those leading out should seek to allow their decisions to be guided, insofar as possible, by the wisdom and insight of the group. As a church, we thus give decision-making authority not to any single president or chairperson, but to committees, where those who lead the group are seeking the wisdom and, where possible, consensus of the group.

God's remnant, then, will treasure a system of church government, authority, and leadership that reflects (as much as is humanly possible) the ideal of God's government of love, within which moral freedom is cherished and leaders are the humble servants of all, even as Christ gave Himself up for all. This very kind of humble servant leadership, grounded in love, was perfectly modeled by Christ who, as unique "head of the church ... loved the church and gave Himself up for her" (Eph. 5:23, 25), supremely exemplifying God's character and moral government of love.

The Unique and Non-Transferrable Headship of Christ

Scripture affirms that the Son is eternally equal with the Father and the Spirit (Col. 2:9; Heb. 1:3; Matt. 28:19; John 1:1; 5:18; 8:58; 14:9; Phil. 2:6; Rom. 9:5; Col. 1:15-17).[6] Scripture also affirms the temporary voluntary functional subordination of Christ the Son in order to accomplish the salvation of humanity (John 5:19; 8:28, 54; 14:10, 28; 17:5; Phil. 2:7-11; Col. 1:18-20; Eph. 1:23; Heb. 1:8; 1 Cor. 15:20-28; Isa. 9:6-7; Dan. 7:13-14; Rev. 11:15).[7] The interpersonal relationships within the Trinity provide the ultimate model of love and self-sacrifice for us. As such, they do not furnish a model for a top-down governmental structure for human leadership within the church.

According to Scripture, Christ is the only head of the church, and the human members of Christ's church collectively (male and female) make up the body of Christ (Eph. 1:22-23; 5:23; Col. 1:18; 2:19; cf. 1 Cor. 11:3; Col. 2:10). Likewise, Ellen White counsels: "Christ, not the

Appendix A

minister, is the head of the church"[8] and "Christ is the only Head of the church."[9] Neither Scripture nor the writings of Ellen White apply the language of headship in the church to anyone other than Christ. Further, neither Scripture nor the writings of Ellen White endorse any transfer of the role of head in the home to roles within the church body.

Since Christ is the only head of the church, no other can be head of the church. That is, headship in the church is unique to Christ and is non-transferrable. All those who would follow Christ's method of ministry cannot do so by taking on His role of headship in the church, but by serving others in accordance with the "mind of Christ" (cf. Phil. 2:5) and God's moral government of love. Deviation from the unique headship of Christ in the church follows the enemy's practice of domination and counterfeit government, which directly contradicts and opposes God's moral government of love.

Accordingly, the role of "head" in the home (Eph. 5:23) is not transferrable to the realm of the church. Indeed, the idea that the role of "head" in the home would or should transfer to other realms is a fallacious *non sequitur* (that is, the transfer from one realm to another does not follow logically). For example, one's role in the home obviously does not translate into a similar or analogous role in one's workplace.

Beyond the logical problems inherent in the move from head of the home to headship in the church, two demonstrably biblical rationales exclude such a transfer. First, as already noted, Christ is the *only* head of the church. Any attempt at proliferation of "heads" in the church is thus unacceptable, for it is a step toward usurping the unique headship role of Christ, who is the only mediator between God and humans. It is unscriptural to speak of any kind of headship in the church apart from that of Christ.

No inspired writer teaches the headship of man over woman at the creation. Rather, Genesis 1 teaches us that male and female participate equally in the image of God, with no hint of pre-Fall subordination of one to the other (1:27). Genesis 2 reinforces Genesis 1 in this regard. Eve's creation from Adam's side shows that she is "to stand by his side

Questions and Answers About Women's Ordination

as an equal" (2:21-22).[10] Although various interpretations of Genesis 3:16 have recognized some kind of post-Fall disruption of this pre-Fall egalitarian ideal, the Bible consistently calls us back to God's original plan for full equality without hierarchy (Song 7:10; Isa. 65:17, 25; cf. Gen. 1:29-30). Paul's writings, though often misunderstood (2 Pet. 3:16), maintain this Eden model (Eph. 5:21-23), affirming with the rest of Scripture the gospel ideal of the ultimate restoration of the Eden model (cf. Matt. 19:8; 2 Cor. 5:17; Gal. 3:28). Ellen White also underlines this redemptive paradigm: "Woman should fill the position which God originally designed for her, as her husband's equal."[11] "The Lord desires His ministering servants to occupy a place worthy of the highest consideration. In the mind of God, the ministry of men and women existed before the world was created."[12] "Infinite wisdom devised the plan of redemption, which places the race on a second probation by giving them another trial."[13]

Second, every member of the church is part of the body of Christ, who is the one head. Since each member of the church (male or female) is a part of the body of Christ, a member cannot at the same time exercise headship in the church. In the same way, since Christ is the unique husband of the church (Christ's metaphorical bride), the members of the church cannot themselves be husbands of the church, but collectively, men and women together are the bride of Christ. That the church as family of God is analogous to human families only serves to suggest that humans should manifest the love of God in their family relationships even as Christ does in relationship to His bride.

Within the body of Christ, the only head of the church, every member of the church body receives spiritual gifts: the Spirit gives to "each one [*hekastos*] individually just as He wills" (1 Cor. 12:11). The Holy Spirit is given to all believers at the time of the end: "And afterwards, I will pour out my Spirit on all people. Your sons and daughters will prophesy, your old men will dream dreams, your young men will see visions. Even on my servants, both men and women, I will pour out my Spirit in those days" (Joel 2:28-30, NIV). Within this very context,

Appendix A

Scripture emphatically excludes the notion of elitism within the church body of Christ, proclaiming that "we were all baptized into one body, whether Jews or Greeks, whether slaves or free, and we were all made to drink of one Spirit. For the body is not one member, but many" (1 Cor. 12:13-14; cf. Gal. 3:28). Thus, no member of the body is "any the less *a part* of the body" regardless of one's role (1 Cor. 12:15-16) and, indeed, those who are deemed "less honorable, on these we bestow more abundant honor" (12:23). In all this, every gift and ministry is nothing without love, for "the greatest of these is love" (1 Cor. 13:13; cf. all of chapter 13; cf. Rom. 12:3-10; Eph. 4:11-16). Here again, the unselfish love that is central to God's moral government should be reflected in humble service to one another within Christ's body and bride, the church.

This is reflected in Seventh-day Adventist Fundamental Belief No. 14, "Unity in the Body of Christ," which reads in part: "The church is one body with many members, called from every nation, kindred, tongue, and people. In Christ we are a new creation; distinctions of race, culture, learning, and nationality, and differences between high and low, rich and poor, male and female, must not be divisive among us. We are all equal in Christ, who by one Spirit has bonded us into one fellowship with Him and with one another; we are to serve and be served without partiality or reservation."[14]

There is no third category between the head and body of Christ, or between the corresponding bridegroom (Christ) and bride (the church). The minister is not to be separate from the body of Christ, but is likewise a member of Christ's body and thus plays a non-elitist role in service to and alongside the other members that corresponds to the individual's Spirit-bestowed gifts and accords with the priesthood of all believers (1 Pet. 2:5-9; Rev. 1:6; 5:10; cf. Ex. 19:5-6). Because it is the Spirit who gives gifts to each one (male and female) as He wills (1 Cor. 12:11; cf. 12, 18, 19, 27-31; Joel 2:28-29; Acts 2:18; Rom. 12:4-8; Eph. 4:11-12; 1 Pet. 4:10), the church confers no spiritual powers or gifts on anyone but merely recognizes the gifts that God has granted and

Questions and Answers About Women's Ordination

facilitates corresponding opportunities for ministry within the body of Christ. Leadership ministries within the church are facilitated by the church body as a recognition of the particular Spirit-given gifts and characteristics of servant leadership that reflect God's moral government of unselfish love (cf. Phil. 2:5-8). In this way, both individually and collectively the church is to complete its mission of proclaiming the three angels' messages and revealing God's character of love, the last revelation of God's mercy to the world.[15]

In sum, any form of headship claimed by a mere human, whether male or female, usurps the sole headship of Christ over the church. Christian service, including church leadership, is to reflect but never usurp Christ's leadership. Thus, while Christ's *manner of* leadership is to be reflected by believers, Christ's *particular role* of leadership is unique and not to be encroached upon by any mere human. Christ alone is the head of the church body, of which all Christians are members and submitted to Him.

No human leader, then, may rightfully assume a headship role within the church; the highest level that any leaders can "ascend" corresponds directly to the depths to which they are willing to descend in loving and humble service, giving themselves for Christ's body even as Christ gave himself for his body and bride, his beloved church, the object of "His supreme regard."[16]

Affirmations and Denials

1. We affirm that there is only one head of the church, Christ, and this headship in the church is non-transferrable and inimitable. Thus, Christ's particular role of leadership is unique.
2. We deny that any human can rightly assume a headship role within the church.
3. We affirm that leadership in the church should be modeled after Christ's servant leadership and grounded in love, with the recognition that Christ's manner of leadership is to be reflected by Christian leaders.

Appendix A

4. We deny any church government that results in sacramental, elitist, and headship-oriented leadership, which are counterfeits of Christ's moral government of love and usurp His unique role and authority as head of the church (His body) and husband of the church (His wife).
5. We affirm that church leaders possess stewardship responsibilities of the affairs of the church, carrying out the decisions of the church made in committee and business sessions.
6. We deny that any mere human is invested with final decision-making authority in regard to church teaching, ritual, or doctrine.
7. We affirm the priesthood of all believers and that no human mediator is needed between God and humans.
8. We deny any elevation of church leaders as mediators between God and humans or as head of or within the church.

---

1. Compare Ellen G. White, *The Desire of Ages* (Mountain View, CA: Pacific Press, 1898), p. 758; *Testimonies for the Church*, Vol. 2 (Mountain View, CA: Pacific Press, 1871), p. 211.
2. Unless indicated otherwise, all Bible quotations are from the *New American Standard Bible* (La Habra, California: Foundation Press Publications, publisher for the Lockman Foundation, 1971), updated edition, 1995.
3. Compare White, *That I May Know Him* (Washington, DC: Review and Herald, 1964), p. 366.
4. See also White, *The Acts of the Apostles* (Mountain View, CA: Pacific Press, 1911), pp. 359-360; *The Desire of Ages* (Mountain View, CA: Pacific Press, 1898), p. 817.
5. It is worth noting that some statements that refer to leadership roles within the church use language that many English versions translate as "rule." For example, 1 Timothy 5:17 states: "The elders who rule [*proestōtes*, from the root *proistemi*] well are to be considered worthy of double honor, especially those who work hard at preaching and teaching" (cf. the similar use of this root in Rom. 12:8; 1 Thess. 5:12; 1 Tim. 3:4-5, 12). The root *proistemi*, here translated "rule," literally refers to those who "stand before," beneficially leading and ministering to the community, and should not be confused with some kind of monarchical rulership or sovereignty. In the LXX it refers to the household "ministry" of a servant of the prince (2 Sam. 13:17; cf. 1 Tim. 3:4-5, 12) and the noun form of this root, *prostatis*, refers to Phoebe's ministry as *diakonos* (Rom. 16:1-2).

Questions and Answers About Women's Ordination

6. See also White, *The Desire of Ages* (Mountain View, CA: Pacific Press, 1898), pp. 469, 530; *The Great Controversy Between Christ and Satan* (Mountain View, CA: Pacific Press, 1911), p. 495; Ellen G. White Comments, *Seventh-day Adventist Bible Commentary*, Vol. 7A (Washington, DC: Review and Herald, 1970), pp. 437-440; *Testimonies to Ministers and Gospel Workers* (Mountain View, CA: Pacific Press, 1923), p. 252; *The Truth About Angels* (Boise, ID: Pacific Press, 1996), p. 209; *Review and Herald*, April 5, 1906.

7. See also White, *Patriarchs and Prophets* (Washington, DC: Review and Herald, 1890), p. 34; *Review and Herald*, Oct. 29, 1895; *Review and Herald*, June 15, 1905; *The Faith I Live By* (Washington, DC: Review and Herald, 1958), p. 76.

8. White, *The Signs of the Times*, Jan. 27, 1890.

9. White, *Manuscript Releases*, Vol. 21 (Silver Spring, MD: Ellen G. White Estate, 1993), p. 274. Compare *The Desire of Ages* (Mountain View, CA: Pacific Press, 1898), p. 817; *The Great Controversy Between Christ and Satan* (Mountain View, CA: Pacific Press, 1911), p. 51.

10. Compare White, *Patriarchs and Prophets* (Washington, DC: Review and Herald, 1890), p. 46.

11. White, *The Adventist Home* (Washington, DC: Review and Herald, 1952), p. 231.

12. White, *Manuscript Releases*, Vol. 18 (Silver Spring, MD: Ellen G. White Estate, 1990), p. 380.

13. White, *Testimonies for the Church*, Vol. 3 (Mountain View, CA: Pacific Press, 1875), p. 484. Compare *Patriarchs and Prophets* (Washington, DC: Review and Herald, 1890), pp. 58-59; *Testimonies for the Church*, Vol. 1 (Mountain View, CA: Pacific Press, 1868), pp. 307-308.

14. See http://www.adventist.org/fileadmin/adventist.org/files/articles/official-statements/28Beliefs-English.pdf

15. White, *Christ's Object Lessons* (Washington, DC: Review and Herald, 1900), p. 415.

16. White, *Sermons and Talks*, Vol. 2 (Silver Spring, MD: Ellen G. White Estate, 1994), p. 215.

Appendix B

A Short History of the Headship Doctrine in the Seventh-day Adventist Church[1]

Chapter One: Questions

The modern "headship principle," which was discussed extensively in the Seventh-day Adventist Church during meetings of the 2013-2014 General Conference Theology of Ordination Study Committee (GC TOSC), may be new truth or it may be new heresy, but it is definitely new.

Though I was born into a conservative Adventist family in 1943, attended Adventist schools from first grade through seminary, and have been employed by the church as a minister for 46 years, I had never heard the headship principle taught in the Adventist Church until 2012, when two areas (unions) of the United States called special business sessions to consider ordaining women to ministry.

This does not mean I grew up in a local congregation where seeing a woman in the pulpit would have seemed normal. After World War II, especially, women were limited largely to domestic duties. Culture dictated that women rarely served as physicians, police officers, lawyers, pilots, truck drivers, construction workers, college presidents, sports figures, or in a host of other roles that were thought of as primarily "male." But Adventist churches had no set of Bible studies—no theology—to support the exclusion of women from pastoral ministry.

When several Adventist ministers began talking about the "headship principle" in 2012, I started asking lifetime Adventist friends if

Questions and Answers About Women's Ordination

they had ever heard of the headship principle before. A well-known pastor with a doctorate in New Testament theology, a member of the GC TOSC, gave the same answer as nearly everyone I asked: "No. Never."

One person gave a different answer. A lifetime Adventist, now retired after many years of teaching at Walla Walla University, told me that he had heard male headship preached by a lay member in a small country church in the 1980s.

It is not just church employees or trained theologians who have never heard headship theology taught by Adventists. A headship advocate on the independent Adventist website, Advindicate.com, blames a conspiracy for the headship principle never being mentioned in Adventist churches:

> "I don't know about you, but whenever I read the Bible and come across one of those many statements on male headship in the home and the church, it seems like my private secret, a secret that I've stumbled upon despite the very best efforts of my church to hide it from me. I always think, 'Wow! I've never heard any Adventist pastor discuss this before.'"[2]

In this study we will see that "the headship principle" is, in fact, new to Seventh-day Adventists in all parts of the world. Today's popular male headship theology was developed in North America by a few Calvinist Evangelical teachers and preachers in the 1970s and 1980s, imported into the Adventist Church in the late 1980s by Andrews University professor Samuele Bacchiocchi (1938-2008), and championed among Adventists during the late 20th and early 21st centuries by a small but committed group of Adventist headship advocates, mostly based in Michigan.

Chapter Two: What Is the Headship Principle?

The foundations for the modern "headship principle" are two Bible passages written by Paul. Those texts are, of course, not new. Paul mentions to Christians in two cities in Asia Minor that man is head of

Appendix B

woman. In 1 Corinthians 11:3 he says, "The head of every man is Christ, the head of woman is man, and the head of Christ is God." And in Ephesians 5:22-23ff., he tells Christians they should all "submit to one another" and then illustrates this by telling wives to "submit to your own husbands, as to the Lord. For the husband is head of the wife, as also Christ is head of the church." He balances that advice with: "Husbands, love your wives, just as Christ also loved the church and gave Himself for her."

Those texts have always been in the New Testament. But what do they mean? How is the headship of men, or of husbands, to be applied today? The modern "headship principle" is one of many possible answers to that question.

Seventh-day Adventists, like other Christians, have never talked much about these headship texts. According to the online index, Ellen White, who wrote about the Bible for more than 70 years, never quoted Paul's statement in 1 Corinthians 11:3 that "the head of woman is man."[3] Paul's point in 1 Corinthians 11 was that women should not cut their hair and they should adorn their heads suitably. Like other Christians, most Adventists have believed that long hair and head coverings were local cultural requirements in Paul's time, but not in ours. When those cultural issues went away, Paul's headship argument was sort of orphaned—an argument without an apparent application.

Paul's counsel to the Ephesians that all Christians, especially husbands and wives, are to submit to one another in love, has not usually been controversial. Ellen White, co-founder of the Seventh-day Adventist Church, who had much to say about the relationship between husbands and wives, mentioned this text 14 times, almost always affirming that the husband is the leader or head of the family but urging mutual love, mutual respect, mutual support, and mutual submission of husbands and wives.

In 1957, the *Seventh-day Adventist Bible Commentary* took this approach when commenting on Ephesians 5:

> "The supreme test of love is whether it is prepared to forgo

Questions and Answers About Women's Ordination

happiness in order that the other might have it. In this respect, the husband is to imitate Christ, giving up personal pleasures and comforts to obtain his wife's happiness, standing by her side in the hour of sickness. Christ gave himself for the church because she was in desperate need; He did it to save her. Likewise the husband will give himself for the salvation of his wife, ministering to her spiritual needs, and she to his, in mutual love."[4]

While men dominated both society and the church for thousands of years, Paul's headship statements were not developed into the modern headship principle until the late 20th century.

In North America in the 1970s and 1980s, several Evangelical Calvinist theologians (also known as Reformed theologians) developed a detailed system of patriarchy, which organizes almost all human relationships around authority and submission—which they call the "headship principle." The modern headship movement is most common where it developed—among Calvinist churches. Like Calvinism itself, it is found most often in Presbyterian and some Southern Baptist Churches. Outside the Adventist denomination, the headship movement is closely identified with the American Christian homeschool movement.[5] Websites that sell homeschool materials often sell materials promoting headship theology.[6]

While no single authority controls headship theology, the Council on Biblical Manhood and Womanhood (CBMW),[7] a Calvinist organization based in Wheaton, Illinois, co-founded by Wayne Grudem and John Piper, is the best-known and most influential organization that develops and promotes headship theology. The most authoritative document of the headship movement is the Danvers Statement, drafted by CBMW in 1987.[8]

The belief that the husband is head of the family, by itself, is not the modern "headship principle"—which includes several additional elements. While not everyone who accepts headship theology agrees on every theological point, and many may not agree with some of the

Appendix B

points below, the following characteristics of headship theology are common among both Calvinist and Adventist proponents. When we say in this paper that headship theology did not exist in the Adventist Church before 1987, the following points are what Adventists did not teach:

- The belief that Adam's headship in marriage was established by God before the Fall, not as a result of sin,[9] and that God created Eve to be subservient to Adam.[10]
- The belief that Christ is eternally in voluntary submission to God the Father, though still fully God.[11]
- The belief that Eve's sin was not so much in trying to become like God as in trying to escape her subordinate "helper" role, and become like Adam.[12]
- The belief that Adam's primary sin was in not exercising authority and leadership over Eve, but letting her lead him, thus reversing the roles they believe were assigned by God.[13]
- The belief that last-day reformation requires that the original pre-sin roles be restored, with men learning "godly headship" (the role that Adam failed to exercise) and women learning "godly submission" (the role that Eve rejected).[14] (In contrast to this, people who believe that Adam's authority over Eve was the result of sin usually believe revival and reformation should include the restoration of pre-sin equality.)
- The belief that the church is an extension of the family and that pastors and church administrators are authorities over members. Therefore, it is a sin for women to serve as pastors, elders, authoritative teachers, or denominational leaders.[15]
- Polarizing language. Advocates of headship theology almost always express their ideas in ways that allows for no other belief or practice.[16] They talk about biblical manhood, biblical womanhood, biblical family structure, biblical headship, biblical authority, biblical submission, biblical methods of child discipline,

Questions and Answers About Women's Ordination

etc. Any relationship of husbands and wives that is not built on authority of the male and submission of the female is, by definition, unbiblical. Women teaching Bible to adult males is unbiblical. The only alternative to biblical submission is rebellion. And the only alternative to biblical headship theology is feminism, which they associate with liberalism, secularism, and homosexuality.

- A fondness among headship scholars for the word *ontological,* a Greek word used to describe the true nature of something.[17] Headship advocates argue that teaching that Christ is eternally and voluntarily subordinate to God the Father is not heresy because Christ, in their view, is ontologically equal to the Father. The belief that Eve was created subordinate to Adam is not unbiblical because she was created ontologically equal to Adam. And Paul's statement that Jews and Gentiles, men and women, slaves and free are all one in Christ is only ontologically (and soteriologically) true: women still cannot be leaders in the church because that would make them authorities over men. (And slavery, according to many headship advocates, is not contrary to Christian teaching, as long as slaves are recognized as ontologically equal to their owners and as long as their owners treat them according to biblical instructions for slave-owners.)[18]
- The belief that God requires that women be removed from leadership positions in churches and the belief that people who do not accept these changes are in rebellion against God.[19] Critics in Calvinist churches and seminaries frequently state that the introduction of headship theology has caused division in many congregations and in several denominations in the United States.[20]
- The belief that it is wrong to accept women into ministerial training courses and then deny them jobs. So religious colleges and seminaries should create separate training programs to train women for roles suitable for women.[21] When, for example, the

Appendix B

Southern Baptist Convention formally adopted the Danvers Statement, several Baptist seminaries were dramatically reorganized, resulting in the loss of many professors.[22]

It is beyond the scope of this paper to examine whether or not the Bible supports the headship doctrine, but in-depth biblical studies are available.[23]

Chapter Three: Adventists Have Never Taught Headship Theology

The modern headship doctrine was unknown in the Adventist Church (or the Christian church) before the 1970s, and it never appeared in any published book or article written by an Adventist before 1987.[24]

Headship theology is not found, for example, in the Seventh-day Adventist Fundamental Beliefs, which were adopted by the General Conference in session in 1980. If Adventists had always believed the headship doctrine, as some advocates claim, and if the headship principle defines all relationships in the home and the church, its absence from the Fundamental Beliefs is difficult to explain.

The Fundamental Belief on Marriage and the Family could easily have said that at creation God assigned to the husband the role of benevolent leader, and to the wife and children the roles of cheerfully submitting to his leadership. Instead, Fundamental Belief No. 23 says about marriage: "Mutual love, honor, respect and responsibility are the fabric of this relationship, which is to reflect the love, sanctity, closeness, and permanence of the relationship between Christ and His church," and "God blesses the family and intends that its members shall assist each other toward complete maturity."

And the Fundamental Belief on Unity in the Body of Christ (No. 14) does not say that unity in the church is based on following the headship principle, with men leading and women following. Instead, this belief says: "In Christ we are a new creation; differences between

Questions and Answers About Women's Ordination

... male and female, must not be divisive among us. We are all equal in Christ, who by one Spirit has bonded us into one fellowship with Him and with one another; we are to serve and be served without partiality or reservation."

The Fundamental Belief on Spiritual Gifts and Ministries (No. 17) does not suggest there is a difference between the gifts God gives to men and those He gives to women, and the Fundamental Belief on Christian behavior says nothing about being subject to authorities.

Clearly, if the Seventh-day Adventist Church had believed in the headship principle in 1980 when the Fundamental Beliefs were first adopted, or at any time since, we should find some hint of that theology in the Fundamental Beliefs. Instead we find the opposite.

But the absence of headship theology in the Fundamental Beliefs is a small part of its absence from church documents. There is also no trace of headship theology in the 900-page *General Conference Working Policy*, the *Church Manual*, the *Ministers Manual*, or the *Official Statements* voted by the General Conference and published on the General Conference website. The headship doctrine is absent from the *Seventh-day Adventist Bible Commentary*, the *Seventh-day Adventist Encyclopedia*, the *Seventh-day Adventist Bible Dictionary*, and the *Seventh-day Adventist Bible Students' Sourcebook*.[25] There is no mention of the headship principle on Seventh-day Adventist baptismal certificates, in the Voice of Prophecy Discover Bible lessons, or in Adventist textbooks for any level of education. And I have found no mention of modern headship theology in Sabbath School quarterlies or in any book or article written by any Adventist pioneer.

The extensive bibliography in Bacchiocchi's anti-women's-ordination book, *Women in the Church*, lists no supporting Adventist references. And later books condemning women's ordination list no sources before Bacchiocchi's book. Current anti-women's-ordination websites that offer publications for further study offer nothing written by Adventists before Bacchiocchi's 1987 book.[26]

Proponents of headship theology, including Bacchiocchi, do quote

Appendix B

texts from the Bible and statements by Ellen White that they believe support headship theology, but they don't quote or list any Adventist teacher or minister before the 1980s who understood those texts and statements to teach headship theology.

Before the development of the headship doctrine in the 1970s and 1980s, there were arguments against women in church leadership and arguments against ordaining women to ministry, but they were not headship arguments and they were usually used *against* Seventh-day Adventists, not *by* Seventh-day Adventists. For example, the argument that "all 12 disciples were male so all ministers today must be male" is part of the argument that the church today should be restored to exactly what the church was like in the New Testament. That is a restorationist argument, not a headship argument. It is an argument that Adventists rejected in the mid-19th century when they chose a name and elected officers. Advocates of headship theology argue that the 12 apostles were all male because of the headship principle, but the restorationist argument existed on its own long before headship theology was developed.

Paul's instructions that women should keep silent in church and that a bishop should be the husband of one wife are not headship texts; they are used by modern advocates of headship theology to illustrate that male headship is a biblical principle, but for more than 100 years before modern headship theology was developed, those texts were used by critics to condemn the Seventh-day Adventist Church for recognizing Ellen White as a spiritual authority. They were not used by Adventists to show that women should submit to men.

Before we examine how early headship theology was introduced to the Adventist Church by Calvinist teacher Bill Gothard, and later adopted from several other Calvinist theologians by Bacchiocchi and others, we need to take a quick look at Calvinism to see why the earliest headship advocates were Calvinists.

Questions and Answers About Women's Ordination

Chapter Four: Calvinism and Headship Theology

It was not an accident that headship theology was developed by Calvinists.

During the 16th century, Protestant theologian John Calvin taught what Adventists usually refer to as predestination, the belief that God "elects" who will be saved and who will be lost and that there is nothing anyone can do to change the decision God has made. In this regard, Calvin's teaching was similar to that of Martin Luther and to Catholic theologian Augustine.[27] Calvin, Luther, and Augustine all taught that God knew from eternity past whether each person would be lost or saved and that God's foreknowledge *determines* ultimate destinies: there is nothing any person can do to change what God has always known. Calvin's "double predestination" was more direct, teaching that God actively *elects* some to be saved and *elects* others to burn eternally in the fires of hell.

Seventh-day Adventists are not Calvinists, or Lutherans, but Arminians.[28] Jacobus Arminius believed that God does not consign anyone to be lost without any choice on his or her part. He believed that predestination makes God a dictator and the author of evil, not at all like Jesus. He taught that the grace of God makes it possible for "whosoever will" to be saved.

The free will theology of Arminius—after being made even "freer" by the founder of Methodism, Charles Wesley—forms the foundation of Seventh-day Adventist Wesleyan-Arminian theology. In her book *The Great Controversy*, Ellen White tells of the millennia-long battle between religion that is based on force and of the true religion of love, which is based entirely on free choice.[29]

What does all this have to do with headship theology? Just this: our view of God determines how we understand Paul's words in 1 Corinthians 11:3, "But I want you to know that the head of every man is Christ, the head of woman is man, and the head of Christ is God."

If God makes all the choices, as Calvin taught, and humans can only submit, then when Paul says that man is the head of woman—like

Appendix B

God the Father is the head of Christ, and like Christ is the head of man—then male "headship" is all about authority and submission. In this version of Calvinist theology, men are given no choice but to submit to the decisions of Christ, so women are given no choice but to submit to the decisions of men. Modern marriage classes based on the headship principle, such as Wayne Grudem's "The Art of Marriage," are designed to teach men how to lead firmly but fairly and to teach women and children how to submit cheerfully and with thanksgiving. But the principle is the same: wives submit to the God-given authority of husbands.

Some people who approach 1 Corinthians 11 and Ephesians 5 with these Calvinist (or sometimes even Lutheran or Catholic) presuppositions see that the submission of women to men is the "plain and obvious" meaning of the text. In the modern headship formula, a God who makes men's most important decisions is reflected by a husband who makes his family's most important decisions.

But as Andrews University professor Darius Jankiewicz explains, if you believe, as Arminians do, that Christ's part in salvation was entirely voluntary from beginning to end; if you believe that Christ freely chose to suffer and die to save everyone, because He loves everyone, but then He exerts no pressure of any kind to force submission; then it follows that men's "headship" of women, like Christ's headship of men, is sacrificial service without any hint of mandatory submission or hint of violating free will.[30] Seventh-day Adventists have taught for decades that without genuine free will, real love—whether for God, for men, or for women—is not possible.

When Arminians read 1 Corinthians 11:3-16, they do not see a system of authority and submission. Instead, they see Paul correcting a problem with arrogant and disruptive women in Corinth. They see instructions for a husband to tenderly protect, nurture, and submit to ("prefer") the decisions of his wife, as Christ tenderly nurtures the church. And an Arminian sees a wife lovingly supporting, respecting, nurturing, and submitting to ("preferring") the decisions of her husband. Instead of moving from 1 Corinthians 11:3 to theories of headship and submission, an Arminian is more likely to move to 1 Corinthians 13 and other texts that tell people how to love and serve each other as Christ loves us.

The modern headship doctrine, which appears to some (but not most) Calvinists as the plain and obvious meaning of Paul's counsel to the believers in Corinth and Ephesus, does not appear at all to most other Christians.[31]

Headship theology played no part in Adventist thought until the late 20th century, when flyers began to arrive for Bill Gothard's seminars.

Chapter Five: Bill Gothard's Chain of Command

In the 1970s, hundreds—possibly thousands—of Seventh-day Adventist youth, youth leaders, teachers, and parents attended the enormously popular Institute in Basic Life Principles seminars conducted by Bill Gothard,[32] then a Wheaton College (Calvinist) professor.

The key phrase in Gothard's pioneering version of headship theology was "God's chain-of-command." One illustration showed God holding a hammer (identified as "father") in His left hand. The hammer pounds on a chisel ("mother") in his right hand, and the point of the chisel chips imperfections off a diamond ("teen-ager"). Notes around the illustration said: "God is able to accomplish His purposes in our lives through those he places over us" and "When a teen-ager reacts against the 'tools' God brings upon his life, he is, in fact, reacting against God himself."

Over every person on earth, God has assigned authorities. The authorities relay God's guidance and protection. For a teen, the highest authority is his or her father. For a wife, it is her husband. The father delegates some authority to the teen's mother, teachers, school principal, employer, government, police, etc. A teen is to submit to all of them to the extent that the father directs. Each authority becomes a link in the chain of command, all under the authority of the father.

Appendix B

In Gothard's success stories, if a young person decided to become a Christian, be baptized, and attend church every week, but the young person's non-Christian father told him or her to have nothing to do with Christianity, the youth was to obey the father. Of course, this created a conflict with the commandment of Jesus to obey God rather than man, but Gothard had two answers: "How big is your God?" and the "creative alternative."

"How big is your God?" meant that regardless of how hard-hearted your father (or husband, teacher, or employer, etc.) might be, God could change that person's decision. So, for Gothard, if the person in authority over you asked you to do something you believed was contrary to God's will, you were to obey the person over you anyway (unless he asked you to commit some clear moral sin like worshipping an idol or killing someone); God was just testing your level of trust. While obeying the authority, the youth (or wife) should look for a "creative alternative," a way to let the authority know you would be loyal and submissive, yet encourage the authority to change his mind and give you permission to do God's will. Daniel's suggestion that Nebuchadnezzar test the Hebrew diet was an example of a creative alternative.

When Adventist youth leaders and ministers repeated Gothard's chain of command theology in Adventist boarding schools, they (we) sometimes created serious questions in the minds of students who had come to the school to escape religious conflict at home. Some had been kicked out of their homes for becoming Christians or Adventists. They had given testimonies at school about how God had taken care of them when they courageously obeyed Him, but now they wondered if they should leave school, ask their parents for forgiveness, and only practice Christianity and/or keep the Sabbath when their parents told them to.

Gothard taught the same submission to the government. That was an emotional topic in the early 1970s, when many church youth were protesting the Vietnam War and considering avoiding military service by hiding, claiming conscientious objection, or fleeing to Canada. Gothard's answer: God placed the government over you. The government's

Questions and Answers About Women's Ordination

laws are God's laws. Do you trust God? If God wants you to not join the army, He will fix things so you don't have to join, but only after He sees that you trust Him enough to join when required.

I was intrigued at the time by the fact that Gothard's headship teaching appeared to be countered almost word for word by Ellen White in *The Great Controversy*, where she wrote about persecution in the final days before the coming of Christ:

> "The miracle-working power manifested through spiritualism will exert its influence against those who choose to obey God rather than men. Communications from the spirits will declare that God has sent them to convince the rejecters of Sunday of their error, affirming that the laws of the land should be obeyed as the law of God" (p. 590).

By the mid-1970s, the war had ended, there was no more military draft, the hippie movement was dead, and Adventists (and other Christians) mostly lost interest in Gothard's chain of command. There may have been hundreds—possibly thousands—of Adventists who were now comfortable with headship theology, but there was no issue in the church that brought it to the surface again until feminism and the ordination of women became issues in the 1980s.

But headship theology was not dead. In the late 1970s and 1980s, Calvinist theologians Wayne Grudem, James B. Hurley, and John Piper emerged as leading developers and proponents of a rejuvenated headship theology, and their writings largely define the headship doctrine among Calvinists and some Adventists in the 21st century.[33] In the early 21st century, Adventist churches frequently offer marriage seminars, parenting seminars, and youth training camps based on the headship theology of Grudem, Hurley, and Piper.[34]

Chapter Six: Samuele Bacchiocchi and *Adventists Affirm*

In 1986, the General Conference published the Mohaven Papers, a collection of study documents and recommendations from a General Conference-sponsored committee that more than 10 years earlier had

Appendix B

studied the ordination of women to ministry.[35] That General Conference committee reported that there was no biblical reason to not ordain women to ministry and recommended that the church begin actively finding ways to incorporate more women into ministry.

Andrews University professor Samuele Bacchiocchi tells us that he became so concerned about the threat of feminism and the possibility that the church might begin ordaining women to ministry that he canceled a major research project he had started and went looking for biblical arguments that would stop the Adventist Church from voting to ordain women to ministry.[36] His bibliography reveals that he found those arguments in the teachings of a few Calvinist Bible teachers who were at that time developing headship theology. In 1987, Bacchiocchi self-published *Women in the Church*.[37] This groundbreaking book imported the entire headship doctrine from those Evangelical Calvinist writers into the Adventist Church.[38]

Bacchiocchi did not leave us to guess about the source of his headship theology. His book was published with two forewords, both written by the Calvinist theologians who were developing the emerging headship theology: Wayne Grudem and James B. Hurley. Both expressed high praise for Bacchiocchi's book. In his acknowledgments, Bacchiocchi says:

> "Among the hundreds of authors I have read in the preparation of this book, two stand out as the ones who have made the greatest contributions to the development of my thoughts, namely, Prof. Wayne Grudem of Trinity Evangelical Divinity School and Prof. James B. Hurley of Reformed Theological Seminary."

Though Calvinist theology seems like an unlikely fit in the Seventh-day Adventist Church, whose theology, as we have seen, is Wesleyan-Arminian, not Calvinist, the emerging headship doctrine was quickly adopted and championed by a group of Adventist theologians, historians, and writers, mostly residents of southwestern Michigan, who, ironically, said their purpose was to prevent the church from adopting

Questions and Answers About Women's Ordination

new theology. Those early adopters of the emerging headship theology created the journal *Adventists Affirm* (initially titled *Affirm*). The first three issues of *Adventists Affirm*, beginning with Spring 1987, were devoted to promoting headship theology, as were many articles in the months and years that followed.

Evidently, the *Adventists Affirm* group kept a close watch on the Calvinist theologians then developing headship theology. In 1987, the Council on Biblical Manhood and Womanhood, co-founded by Grudem and Piper, drafted what remains today the defining document of the headship movement, the Danvers Statement.[39] The CBMW published the Danvers Statement rather quietly in November 1988, but in January 1989 they attracted much wider attention for the Danvers Statement when they published it as a center spread in Christianity Today.

Almost immediately (Fall 1989), the *Adventists Affirm* group published their own headship statement, using the same presentation style as the Danvers Statement, repeating some of its points and borrowing some of its language.[40] Though the *Adventists Affirm* statement makes many of the same points as the Danvers Statement (e.g., women are equal to men but have been assigned different roles), it is not entirely parallel because the *Adventists Affirm* statement focused more narrowly on the ordination of women, which was by then on the agenda for the 1990 General Conference session in Indianapolis, Indiana.

In 1995, *Adventists Affirm* asked Samuel Koranteng-Pipim, then a doctoral candidate at Andrews University, to write a new book showing that the ordination of women was contrary to Bible teachings. In the decades that followed, Pipim became probably the most well-known and the most quoted advocate for the new headship theology. His initial 96-page book, *Searching the Scriptures*, relied heavily on the same Calvinist writers who had influenced Bacchiocchi. After four chapters outlining church policy and defining the headship doctrine, chapters five and six deal with "Theological Obstacles to Women's Ordination" and "Biblical Obstacles to Women's Ordination." In the first

Appendix B

endnote for chapter five, Pipim says:

> "Those desiring to pursue this subject in greater exegetical and theological detail will greatly benefit from John Piper and Wayne Grudem, eds., *Recovering Biblical Manhood and Womanhood: A Response to Evangelical Feminism*, (Wheaton, Ill., Crossway, 1991). Its exposition of the strengths and some of the weaknesses in the arguments for ordaining women has enriched the study presented here."

In 2000, *Adventists Affirm* published *Prove All Things*, a 424-page book advocating the headship principle. Near the back (pp. 405-412) is a section listing 100 recommended books or articles for further reading. Of the 38 non-Adventist recommendations, 22 are various chapters in *Recovering Biblical Manhood and Womanhood*, edited by Piper and Grudem, and most of the remaining 16 non-Adventist recommended sources are from well-known Calvinist authors and publishers.

Chapter Seven: Changing Culture and Changing Attitudes

While it is clear that Bacchiocchi played a pivotal role in introducing Calvinist headship theology to Adventists, he did not operate in a vacuum. Bacchiocchi's new headship theology seems to have answered a need that was keenly felt in the church in the middle 1980s, a need that had not been felt earlier. If fundamentalism arose in the early 20th century because Christians were alarmed by modern science and liberal theology, and Gothard's teachings were popular in the 1970s because Christians were frightened by cultural upheaval, what happened in American culture between about 1975 and 1985 that causes enough fear to create a market for adopting new theology?

A look at almost any book, paper, or website advocating male headship theology provides a clear answer: the threat of feminism.

Gerhard F. Hasel (1935-1994) provides an interesting illustration. From the 1970s to the early 1990s, Hasel served as professor of Old Testament and biblical theology as well as dean of the Seventh-day Adventist Theological Seminary at Andrews University in Berrien

Questions and Answers About Women's Ordination

Springs, Michigan. In 1973, Hasel presented a scholarly paper to the Mohaven Committee demonstrating that Eve was not created in any way subservient to Adam, that even her role after sin did not include Adam exercising arbitrary authority over her, and that there was nothing in the Bible that precluded women from any leadership roles in the church, including that of ordained minister.[41]

But in 1989, *Adventists Affirm* published an article by Hasel titled "Biblical Authority and Feminist Interpretations," which, without mentioning his earlier position, identified women's ordination with feminist methods of Bible interpretation, which, he said, undermined the authority of the Bible and did away with the Sabbath.[42] Hasel had not even mentioned feminism in his 1973 paper, but after the mid-1980s, Hasel spoke and wrote about the danger of feminist principles of Bible interpretation—symbolized for him by the ordination of women to ministry.[43]

Gordon Hyde underwent a similar change. In 1973, as director of the General Conference Biblical Research Institute, Hyde was asked by the General Conference to establish a committee to study the ordination of women to ministry. He organized the Mohaven committee and served as its secretary. In 1989, Hyde told *Adventists Affirm* readers, "At Mohaven I was an advocate of new opportunities and wider authority for women in the church."[44] Hyde reported at its conclusion that the committee had found no biblical reason to not ordain women to ministry. The Mohaven committee proposed a process that would lead to ordinations of women by 1975.

But in 1989 *Adventists Affirm* published an article by Hyde entitled, "The Mohaven Council—Where It All Began: What Really Happened, and Why the Secretary Has Changed His Mind."[45]

Again, what happened after 1973 that caused Hyde to see old scriptures in a new way?

Not surprisingly, Hasel and Hyde in their later statements mention changes in the intellectual world. Hyde says that "several papers subsequently came in, from individuals whom I highly respect for their

Appendix B

scholarship and their Christian leadership, challenging the assumption by Mohaven that the Scriptures themselves were neutral on the ordination-of-women question." In a few paragraphs, Hyde summarizes the arguments made by Bacchiocchi in his 1987 book, though he does not mention Bacchiocchi by name.

Hasel has much more to say about the biblical reasons for his new position, but most of his new insights were the same as those presented by Bacchiocchi and the Calvinist theologians Bacchiocchi learned from. Hasel references several of the Evangelical theologians that Bacchiocchi lists as contributors to his thinking.

General Conference President Neal C. Wilson also reported a change of attitude during this time. He said during the 1985 General Conference Study Committee meeting in Washington, D.C., that from 1973 to 1975, his position "was more favorable toward ordaining women than it is today." He said he had become "much less certain and increasingly apprehensive regarding where such changes as ordaining women will carry us."[46]

But, why? What happened during the 10 or so years after Mohaven (1973) that made headship theology attractive to Adventists? What caused feminism to look like such a threat to the church that Bacchiocchi's new theology was adopted by Hasel, Hyde, Wilson, and many other conservative Adventists?

The answer is clear. The decade beginning in 1972 saw extraordinary advances in women's rights. No doubt, many Adventists were as alarmed by some of these feminist victories as were other conservative Christians during the 1970s and 1980s.

In 1972, the federal Equal Rights Amendment (ERA) was passed by both houses of Congress. If it had been ratified by 38 states within the 10-year deadline, it would have changed the U.S. Constitution, giving the federal government the power to intervene and stop any discrimination against women in the United States. For more than a decade, Americans in almost every state suffered through months, or years, of political campaigning, with opponents claiming passage of

Questions and Answers About Women's Ordination

the ERA would result in such things as unisex restrooms and drafting women into combat roles in the army. In the end, only 35 states ratified the ERA, so it did not become federal law.

In 1972, "Title IX" ("Title Nine") was added to the Civil Rights Act of 1962, ending public schools' ability to spend more on men's sports programs (or any educational program) than on corresponding women's programs. It was seen by many as a threat to the American way of life—just to satisfy the ambitions of a few shrill women.

More was to come. In 1973, the United States Supreme Court ruled in *Roe v. Wade* that women have a constitutional right to decide whether or not to have an abortion, resulting (in the view of many conservative Christians) in the murder of perhaps a million babies each year—again, to satisfy the ambitions of a few women.

But nothing concerned Adventist Church members and leaders more, or had a wider permanent impact on the church, than the Merikay Silver lawsuits against Pacific Press, demanding equal pay for women. This courtroom drama started at almost the same time (1973) as the Camp Mohaven study and lasted for more than 10 years. Accounts of this crisis are available elsewhere, so we do not need to recount it here, but a short summary will remind us of how it sensitized the church—in a largely negative way—to issues of gender equality.[47]

Before Merikay Silver, church policy enabled almost all Adventist Church entities in the United States—from elementary schools to colleges, hospitals, publishing houses, media ministries and conference offices—to balance their budgets by paying women a lot less than men, even for the same work. If the church in the United States was suddenly required to pay women the same wages as men doing the same jobs, almost all church budgets would be in trouble.

While many Adventists saw Merikay Silver and other female employees as ordinary church members asking to be treated fairly, others saw them as ambitious and greedy, willing to destroy the mission of the church for the cause of feminism. It is difficult to imagine a conflict better designed to create a demand for new theology teaching the

Appendix B

"biblical" submission of women and the different "roles" God had assigned them to play. A summary available from the conservative, independent ministry Pilgrim's Rest illustrates not only the threat that many saw in the Merikay Silver case, but its connection in some minds with the ordination of women to ministry:

> "[In 1985] Merikay betrayed the Press, and exposed it to government interference. . . . The excellent head-of-household plan, which enabled mothers to stay at home with the children was betrayed. All the workers at the Press were betrayed [by Merikay], for seeking to grasp more, many were laid off. . . . The betrayals at Pacific Press soon spread throughout the church in the United States. One effect was layoffs. . . . The reason: The women workers had to be paid more. Many small church schools closed their doors; other workers were laid off. Another effect added momentum to the women's lib movement. It had effectively started in September 1973, when Dr. Josephine Benton joined the Sligo Church in Takoma Park, Maryland, as the first female associate pastor of an American Adventist congregation. In 1980, she became the first American in recent history to serve as senior pastor of a church: the Rockville, Maryland, church. Winning the war on women's wages ... gave great impetus to the 'women's rights' issues in the church. Every year the larger battle—to make women as full-fledged pastors as the men—increases."[48]

Merikay Silver and the Seventh-day Adventist Church settled out of court in 1985, but not before the U.S. Government (EEOC) had won its class action lawsuit, requiring the church to treat women equally in pay and employment practices. In the view of many, probably most Adventists today, paying women the same as men for doing the same job simply made the church a better, more Christlike, place. But for others, the Merikay Silver case meant the church was the victim of an ungodly feminist campaign.

Whether or not the Merikay Silver case was a contributing factor, by the late 1980s feminism was viewed by many Adventists as a threat

Questions and Answers About Women's Ordination

to the mission and survival of the organized church. And many welcomed headship theology as just what the denomination needed to stop feminism's advances.

From 1987 until 2012, headship theology appeared in several independently published Adventist books and sermons written or preached by *Adventists Affirm* board members and contributors, but it almost never appeared in the official publications of the church. One exception was 1995, when the main presentation at the General Conference Session opposing the ordination of women to ministry included elements of the new headship doctrine.[49] That presentation gave headship theology its widest Adventist exposure to that date.

In 2012, when the General Conference assembled 106 people to restudy the theology of ordination and the place of women in ministry, General Conference leaders gave advocates of headship theology equal representation. As a result, the documents posted on the General Conference's Theology of Ordination Study Committee website[50] show that the committee spent a large part of its time debating headship theology, instead of studying the theology of ordination.

It is likely that the Theology of Ordination Study Committee process, with headship theology advocates (and opponents) traveling from North America to meet with the division Biblical Research Committees around the world, and arguing their case at the official meetings, provided the broadest venue to date for the spread of headship theology among Adventists.

Chapter Eight: What's New in Modern Headship Theology?

The modern headship principle, developed by Wayne Grudem, James B. Hurley, John Piper, and others in the 1980s, included two new elements that made it attractive to some Seventh-day Adventists: (1) an upgraded view of the value of women, and (2) new Bible arguments supporting male headship and female submission.

By the 1980s, the old views of women as morally and intellectually inferior, flawed, and incapable of leadership were no longer possible for

Appendix B

Christians, especially in developed nations. Women were beginning to outnumber men on college campuses, outperform men academically in most subjects at all levels of education, and perform well in once male-dominated professions, including medicine, law, business, communication, counseling, politics, and others. If patriarchalism was to survive, it had to be adjusted to present women as just as valuable and capable as men—but assigned different roles by God. The modern headship movement met that need, defining Eve as both equal to Adam (ontologically) and not equal to Adam (functionally). That was new. Though critics consider this idea of "equal but not equal" to be simply self-contradictory and impossible, headship advocates say it makes perfect sense and is God's will.

Viewing women as equally valuable to men called for a new kind of headship and a new kind of submission, with husbands exercising loving and self-sacrificing service to their wives (without giving up authority) and wives offering loving service to their husbands (while recognizing his authority). There is officially no place in the modern headship principle for men abusing or dominating women, though many critics say abuse is an inevitable and common result.

The second innovation proved just as important to Adventists: the arguments that Grudem and Piper created in support of the modernized doctrine of male headship. Before Rushdoony, Grudem, and several other Calvinists created the new headship arguments, Adventists had no set of biblical arguments supporting male headship and female submission.

If you were an Adventist in 1980 and you wanted to prove from the Bible that a woman was forbidden by God to serve as pastor of a local congregation, where would you have started? We have already seen in chapter three that you would not have gotten help from any Adventist denominational publication. Neither could you have turned to independently published Adventist books or articles on the topic, because they hadn't been written yet. So it would be just you and the Bible. Where would you start?

Questions and Answers About Women's Ordination

The most obvious—but problematic—place to start would be with the texts that said women should be silent in church and that women should not teach men. But for more than 120 years, Church of Christ ministers and members had been using those texts to try to prove that Ellen White's preaching and teaching ministry was contrary to the Bible. And for the same period of time, Adventist preachers had been demonstrating that the "keep silent" and "don't teach men" texts dealt with local issues in the first century but did not exclude women from preaching and teaching, either in New Testament times or today. Ellen White, the most prominent co-founder of the Seventh-day Adventist Church, preached in churches regularly and taught religious truth to men her whole life. She preached evangelistic sermons that brought sinners to Christ, and she made passionate speeches at denominational business meetings that resulted in organizational restructuring and institutional development. Clearly these texts would not work for Adventists.

Or you might have started with the texts that said a bishop or deacon should be the husband of one wife and have well-behaved children. But Adventists believed, as indicated in the *Seventh-day Adventist Bible Commentary,* that Paul's intent was to require moral integrity, not to require that elders be men, married, or parents. A literal application of these texts would have excluded both Paul and Jesus from church leadership.

The emerging headship theology offered Adventists a new place to start. The books published independently by Michigan Adventists in the 1980s and early 1990s make it clear that the new headship argument was simple. It had three parts.

The first part of the new argument created an emotional context by talking about the breakdown of society—divorce, immorality, feminism, homosexuality, rock music, etc.—and asserting that those things were all parts of a feminist attack on the Bible and religion. Specifically, they were the results of disregarding the distinct roles they said God has assigned to men and women.

Appendix B

Second, proponents of the headship doctrine began their Bible arguments in Genesis 1-2, asserting that—before sin—God created men to lead and women to submit. They claimed that sin was the result of both Adam and Eve abandoning their assigned roles. All headship theology seems to live or die on this one assertion—an assertion that Adventists had never made. If Eve was created subservient to Adam, then women's submission to men can be seen as a permanent, God-ordained principle. With that point established, the rest of the Bible becomes a collection of illustrations of the headship principle. (By contrast, all denominational publications taught that Eve was created equal to Adam and became subject to his rulership as a result of sin. If that is the case, then the original principle of perfect equality, no matter how difficult to find during much of history, remains the eternal model and a significant goal of redemption and restoration.)

Third, having satisfied themselves that male headship is a permanent principle established before sin, headship advocates, whether Calvinist or Adventist, sweep through the Bible finding illustrations of male headship and female submission almost everywhere: Old Testament priests; New Testament apostles, elders, and deacons; Paul's counsels on women; etc.

And now, since they have already established the male "headship principle," none of these illustrations or texts are required to prove anything. Whether women were Paul's co-workers or not, they still had no authority over men. If women preached and taught and led churches, they didn't have authority over men because that would have been contrary to the principle established in Eden; if all the disciples were men, that illustrates the male headship principle, and it doesn't matter that they were also all Jewish. If in Christ there is no male or female because we are all one in Christ, that is only ontological equality; women still can't serve in the same leadership positions as men because that would be contrary to the principle of male headship established in Eden. If requirements that women wear head coverings, not cut their hair, keep silent in church, and not teach men were all due to local and temporary cultural conditions, these requirements still illustrated temporary expressions of the eternal male headship principle. And now the texts that said bishops and deacons should be the husband of one wife did mean that only men could be church leaders, because that is the principle that was established in Eden. (Of course, marriage and bearing children were also established before sin, but for some reason headship advocates do not insist that ministers be married and have children.)

So the headship principle is a closed system. Once Eve's original, pre-sin role has been defined as submission to Adam, no other argument or text can disprove it. In the judgment of critics of headship theology, the headship doctrine forces some very clear New Testament texts (like Gal. 3:28) to fit into a doubtful and speculative, or even impossible, interpretation of the Creation story. But to its advocates, the headship principle becomes the key to Scripture.

That is what Bacchiocchi and others found new and useful in the Calvinist headship theology that was emerging in the 1980s: first, a new definition of the value of women that fit late 20th century culture, while still denying certain leadership roles; second, the motivation gained from the threat of feminism and confused sex roles; third, a new way of interpreting the Creation story in which Adam and Eve were equal but not equal; and finally, a biblical-sounding eternal "principle" that served as a guide for how every Bible text regarding women was to be interpreted.

Chapter Nine: Conclusion

Before Bacchiocchi and *Adventists Affirm* introduced headship theology to the Adventist denomination in 1987, Adventists had been moving slowly and steadily toward fully integrating women into ministry. This was not a huge issue for a church that was co-founded by a woman—a wife and mother who today remains the highest spiritual authority outside the Bible in the organized church. During the last 50 years, the church has approved the ordination of female elders[51] and deaconesses[52] and has voted that women may serve as "commissioned"

Appendix B

pastors and may perform substantially all the functions of ordained male pastors.[53] In some parts of the world, conferences and unions have begun treating women exactly the same as men, including ordaining women to ministry. And in other parts of the world, where culture prohibits women serving in leadership positions, and where having women pastors would hinder the spread of the gospel, the integration has moved much slower, or not at all. In this, the church may be seen as following Paul's example: "I have become all things to all men, that I might by all means save some" (1 Cor. 9:22, NKJV).

Whenever the General Conference has formed committees in the past to consider ordaining women to ministry, they have found no biblical reasons not to. If Bacchiocchi and others had not brought headship theology into the Seventh-day Adventist Church, study committees in the 21st century would almost certainly be affirming previous committee findings that the leadership of women is in keeping with the principles of the New Testament church. Leaders would be deciding where in the world the ordination of women as pastors would contribute to bringing more people to Jesus and where such a practice would hinder the mission of the church—that is, deciding how to be "all things to all men" in order that by "all means" we might save some.

In his introduction, Bacchiocchi makes it clear that he believed the emerging headship arguments were so powerful that they would unite the church behind a policy that no women could serve as elders or pastors, whether ordained or not. Instead, the new headship doctrine that he introduced seems to be polarizing the Adventist world church over the question of whether or not Seventh-day Adventists will accept the new headship doctrine.

Were it not for the new headship doctrine, the church might have easily adopted a policy of unity in diversity, allowing each division, union, and conference to decide how to incorporate women into ministry. Instead, the church is faced with the difficult task of learning how to relate to a new theology that permits no compromise or diversity.

No one is advocating that Seventh-day Adventists adopt the entire

Questions and Answers About Women's Ordination

package of Calvinist predestination theology. But is it possible to pick just one apple from the Calvinist tree without changing Adventists' traditional understandings of such things as the gracious character of God, the spiritual relationship between Christ and His followers, the commitment to religious liberty for all, and the urgency to take the gospel to every person on earth? That is the question that the Adventist denomination must answer before members and leaders can unite around any ordination theology.

---

1. Copyright © 2014 Gerry Chudleigh. Revised Sept. 1, 2014. Gerry Chudleigh is communication director for the Pacific Union Conference of Seventh-day Adventists, based in Thousand Oaks, Calif., and publisher of the *Pacific Union Recorder*. But the views expressed in this paper are his own, not necessarily those of his employer.

2. David Read, "Are Adventists Coalescing Into Opposing Parties?" (Part I), Advindicate.com, March 24, 2014.

3. See https://egwwritings.org/ (click "Search" and "Scriptural Index").

4. *Seventh-day Adventist Bible Commentary*, Vol. 6 (Washington, DC: Review and Herald, 1957), p. 1035.

5. For example, one of the earliest and most controversial headship theologians, Presbyterian minister R. J. Rushdoony, earned a large part of his income as an expert witness, testifying in support of homeschooling; Bill Gothard redirected his organization almost entirely from headship seminars to homeschool training and supplies, and the Council on Biblical Manhood and Womanhood, the center of Calvinist headship theology, is a major homeschooling resource.

6. While some Adventist homeschool websites, such as http://www.orion-publishing.org, offer books arguing for male headship and against women in ministry, this appears to be because a large number of Adventist homeschoolers are conservative, not because the Adventist Homeschooling movement is rooted in male headship theology.

7. See http://cbmw.org/.

8. Read the full Danvers Statement at http://cbmw.org/core-beliefs/.

9. Danvers Statement, Affirmation No. 3.

10. Gerhard Pfandl, Daniel Bediako, Steven Bohr, Laurel and Gerard Damsteegt, Jerry Moon, Paul Ratsara, Ed Reynolds, Ingo Sorke, and Clinton Wahlen, in "Evaluation of Egalitarian Papers" (paper presented at the Theology of Ordination Study Committee, Jan. 21-25, 2014), p. 4, write: "God appointed Adam as leader in the Garden of Eden before creating the woman."

11. Most Adventist headship advocates are firm that Christ is voluntarily submissive to God the Father. Some are also clear that this is an eternal role distinction. For example, Edwin Reynolds, in "Biblical Hermeneutics and Headship in First Corinthians" (paper presented at the Theology of Ordination Study Committee, Jan. 21-25, 2014), p. 23,

Appendix B

says: "It [voluntary submission] is characteristic of the role relationships between Christ and His Father that extends from eternity past to eternity future."

12. John W. Peters, in "Restoration of the Image of God: Headship and Submission" (paper presented at the Theology of Ordination Study Committee, Jan. 21-25, 2014), p. 17, says: "Eve's hope to be like God was *not* the 'higher sphere' which she sought to enter, nor is that the higher sphere that modern Eves hope to enter. The context suggests that modern Eves hope to enter a higher sphere by attempting to rise above their original positions, by their husband's side."

13. Peters, p. 19, says: "By choosing to take the fruit from Eve and eating the fruit, Adam relinquished his headship role. In effect Adam transferred his headship role to his wife, and the role reversal between Adam and Eve was consummated."

14. Edwin Reynolds and Clinton Wahlen, in "Minority Report" (p. 200 of the North American Division Theology of Ordination Study Committee report), approvingly quote Calvinist theologian Raymond C. Ortland Jr.: "Christian redemption does not redefine creation; it restores creation, so that wives learn godly submission and husbands learn godly headship." From "Male-Female Equality and Male Headship," a chapter in *Recovering Biblical Manhood and Womanhood: A Response to Evangelical Feminism*, edited by John Piper and Wayne Grudem (Wheaton, IL: Crossway, 2006), p. 109.

15. C. Raymond Holmes, in "Women in Ministry: What Should We Do Now?" (paper presented at the Theology of Ordination Study Committee, Jan. 21-25, 2014), p. 12, says: "While the role of women in ministry is unique and 'essential', it is different in function than that of men in that it does not include the headship office and supervising responsibility of elder."

16. Holmes, p. 10, says, "Any solution that would ignore the biblical principle of headship . . . is simply untenable."

17. For example, see Paul Ratsara and Daniel K. Bediako, "Man and Woman in Genesis 1-3: Ontological Equality and Role Differentiation" (paper presented at the Theology of Ordination Study Committee, Jan. 21-25, 2014).

18. See, for example, P. Gerard Damsteegt, Edwin Reynolds, Gerhard Pfandl, Laurel Damsteegt, and Eugene Prewitt, "Interpreting Scripture on the Ordination of Women" (paper presented at the Theology of Ordination Study Committee, Jan. 21-25, 2014), p. 24.

19. Holmes, p. 15, says: "Collectively we have some repenting to do. . . . [Begin by] rescinding all previous actions permitting the ordination of women as local elders. Also, the 1990 General Conference action allowing women to perform most of the functions of an ordained minister in their local churches should be carefully reconsidered."

20. While Calvinist critics of headship theology often mention that headship theology has split many churches, these "splits" are difficult to document because when a congregation, school, or denomination is "split" by the headship theology, a new organization is not usually formed. Those opposed to the new headship demands usually move to an existing congregation, seminary, or denomination that does not teach the modern headship principle. Examples include the local congregation that former President Jimmy Carter left, the Southern Baptist Seminary, and the Southern Baptist

Questions and Answers About Women's Ordination

Convention, all of which retained a core of headship supporters while large numbers of non-supporters left.

21. Holmes, p. 12, says: "As long as women in ministry are trained for the same office and role for which men are trained, they can be expected to claim the same outcome. . . . We do the women God is calling to ministry a terrible disservice as long as we do not provide training for the specific ministry to which God is calling them. It is our failure to provide such training that constitutes unfairness and injustice."

22. On March 10, 2014, Cedarville [Ohio] University President Thomas White announced that due to the concept of headship in 1 Corinthians 11:2-16, the university is restricting classes in the women's ministry program—which some say is every Bible class taught by a woman—to only female students." See http://www.christianitytoday.com/gleanings/2014/march/christian-college-solidifies-complementarian-cedarville.html.

23. Several papers presented at the 2014 Theology of Ordination Study Committee examine the headship doctrine from a biblical perspective. In support: John W. Peters, "Restoration of the Image of God: Headship and Submission." Against: Ángel Manuel Rodríguez, "Evaluation of the Arguments Used by Those Opposing the Ordination of Women to the Ministry" and Kendra Haloviak Valentine, "Is Headship Theology Biblical?" See also Richard M. Davidson, "Headship, Submission, and Equality in Scripture," *Women in Ministry: Biblical & Historical Perspectives*, by a Special Committee of the Seventh-day Adventist Theological Seminary, Nancy Vyhmeister, Ed. (Berrien Springs, MI: Andrews University Press, 1998). Read online at http://session.adventistfaith.org/assets/393498.

24. Historians have noted that in Reformed theology, the subordinate position of women is similar to the position of women in pre-Reformation Catholic theology. One difference is that the older theology usually presented women as weaker spiritually, less intelligent, and more gullible than men, while the new headship theology, following the pioneering headship theologian R. J. Rushdoony, insists that women are not inferior to men but have just been assigned a subordinate functional role.

25. On Genesis 1-3, the *Seventh-day Adventist Bible Commentary* (Washington, DC: Review and Herald, 1957) gives no hint that Adam was head over Eve before sin. On Paul's counsel in 1 Timothy 3, that bishops and deacons should be "the husband of one wife," the commentary lists four possible meanings; that they must be male is not included in the list. To modern readers looking for arguments for or against the headship principle, the comments on the two headship texts, 1 Corinthians 11 and Ephesians 3, look as if they were written by an egalitarian and a headship advocate who took turns writing paragraphs. There is plenty for both sides to love and hate. But the headship doctrine was not developed until a quarter century after the commentary was published, so the authors were not addressing our questions. The commentary affirms that before sin, the authority and rank of Adam and Eve were perfectly equal; that as a result of sin, man has been assigned to be the head, leader, or even "ruler" of the family; that the gospel seeks to restore the relationship of husband and wife to perfect equality; and that in a Christian home, husband and wife will work so diligently for the happiness and benefit of each other—even at the cost of their own lives—that neither will ever think about who is the head. The authors do not connect the headship texts with the issue of which church offices a woman may hold. See especially Vol. 6, pp.

Appendix B

753-759 and pp. 1035-1038.

26. For an example of an anti-ordination website that includes no Adventist references before 1987 but suggests a list of Evangelical Calvinist authors for further study, see http://www.womenministrytruth.com/free-resources/other-insightful-works.aspx.

27. See Brian G. Mattson, "Double or Nothing: Martin Luther's Doctrine of Predestination," 1997, at http://www.contra-mundum.org/essays/mattson/Luther-predestination.pdf.

28. Arminians, who mostly agree with the free-will theology of Jacobus Arminius, are not to be confused with Armenians, citizens of the country of Armenia or people of Armenian ancestry. Nor should Arminianism be confused with Arianism, the belief that Jesus was not eternally and fully God.

29. Woodrow W. Whidden II, in "Grace, Free Will, and Judgment," *Adventist Review*, Oct. 14, 2010, Vol. 187, No. 33, says: "To put it very simply: no 'free grace' and its 'freed wills,' no God-vindicating 'Great Controversy theme' for Seventh-day Adventism!" See http://archives.adventistreview.org/article/3799/archives/issue-2010-1533/grace-free-will-and-judgment.

30. Darius Jankiewicz, "Two Visions of God and Male Headship: A Study in Calvinist and Arminian Presuppositions" (presentation during the 2010 Arminianism Symposium, Oct. 15, 2010).

31. For Evangelical criticism of Calvinist headship theology, see http://www.godswordtowomen.org/headship.htm.

32. In 2014, the website billgothard.com states that more than 2.5 million people have attended Bill Gothard's basic seminar since 1964.

33. Some church historians date the emergence of the modern headship movement from the publication of Wayne Grudem's *Systematic Theology: An Introduction to Biblical Doctrine* (Grand Rapids, MI: Zondervan, 1994).

34. For example, at the time of this writing in early 2014, an Adventist church in the Central California Conference advertised a headship seminar for youth at a lodge in Yosemite, and a church in the Southern California Conference offered "The Art of Marriage," a video seminar for couples featuring the headship teachings of Wayne Grudem.

35. See General Conference Archives at http://www.adventistarchives.org/1973-5-mohaven-.VBR4Xv3gVuY.

36. Samuele Bacchiocchi, *Women in the Church: A Biblical Study of the Role of Women in the Church* (Berrien Springs, MI: Biblical Perspectives, 1987), pp. 11-18.

37. The full text of Bacchiocchi's book *Women in the Church* is available at http://peter.hitechemall.com/english/dnl/bacchi/books/womench.pdf.

38. Bacchiocchi was not the first Adventist in the 1970s or 1980s to express headship ideas. At Camp Mohaven in 1973, Hedwig Jemison presented a collection of statements from Ellen White, with commentary suggesting she had accepted headship theology. And the skeletal minutes from the General Conference's 1985 Role of Women in the Church Committee indicate that at least one unnamed member of the committee was presenting headship arguments. But Bacchiocchi was the first Adventist to compile and

Questions and Answers About Women's Ordination

publish the emerging headship doctrine.

39. Read the full Danvers Statement at http://cbmw.org/core-beliefs/.

40. Read the *Adventists Affirm* Affirmations Statement at http://session.adventistfaith.org/no or in the *Pacific Union Recorder*, August 2012, Vol. 112, No. 8, pp. 44, 46.

    The full Danvers Statement was written in the form of 10 "concerns," followed by 10 "affirmations." Similarly, the full *Adventists Affirm* statement—first published in its Autumn 1989 issue and later reprinted as Appendix B in *Prove All Things: A Response to Women in Ministry*, Mercedes H. Dyer, Ed. (Berrien Springs, MI: *Adventists Affirm*, 2000), pp. 375-381—took the form of 11 "concerns" followed by 10 "affirmations." The following juxtaposition of sentences from the DANVERS STATEMENT, Concern No. 3 (indicated by all capital letters), and the *Adventists Affirm* statement, Concern No. 7 (indicated with italic type), illustrate the way the *Adventists Affirm* group borrowed language, style, and ideas from the Danvers Statement.

    In their statements, both the DANVERS group and the *Adventists Affirm* group OBSERVE WITH DEEP CONCERN (*are deeply concerned over*): "THE INCREASING PROMOTION (*increasing promotion*) GIVEN TO FEMINIST EGALITARIANISM (*of feminist interpretations*) WITH ACCOMPANYING DISTORTIONS OR NEGLECT OF (*which distort*) THE GLAD HARMONY PORTRAYED IN SCRIPTURE (*what the Bible says*) BETWEEN THE LOVING, HUMBLE LEADERSHIP OF REDEEMED HUSBANDS (*about the sacrificial headship role of a caring husband*) AND THE INTELLIGENT, WILLING SUPPORT OF THAT LEADERSHIP (*and the willing helper role*) BY REDEEMED WIVES (*of an intelligent, loving, wife*)."

41. Gerhard F. Hasel, "The Relationship of Man and Woman in the Beginning and at the End" (unpublished manuscript presented at Camp Mohaven, 1973). In the final sentence, Hasel calls for men and women to "participate in full equality of responsibilities and privileges in all lines of work in order to hasten the coming of our beloved Lord and Savior Jesus Christ."

42. *Adventists Affirm*, Autumn 1989, pp. 12-23.

43. One theologian told me that Hasel, before his death, returned to his original position, but Hasel never wrote anything documenting that change.

44. *Ibid.*, p. 42.

45. *Ibid.*, pp. 41-43.

46. Report of the Role of Women in the Church Committee, Mar. 26-29, 1985, p. 18. See http://www.adventistarchives.org/1985-study-committee-minutes.pdf.

47. For the story from Merikay Silver's perspective, see her book, *Betrayal: The Shattering Sex Discrimination Case of Silver Vs. Pacific Press Publishing Association* (Austin, TX: Mars Hill Publications, 1985).

48. See Vance Ferrell, "The Merikay Silver Case" (Part 1 or 3), *Waymarks*, August 1996, p. 12, at http://www.sdadefend.com/MINDEX-M/Silver.pdf.

49. P. Gerard Damsteegt, "A Response to the North American Division Ordination Request," is available online at http://www.andrews.edu/~damsteeg/Ordination.html.

Appendix B

50. See http://www.adventistarchives.org/gc-tosc - .VBS3P_3gVuY.

51. General Conference Committee Minutes, April 3, 1975, 75-153-154, and October 14, 1984, 84-386-387.

52. General Conference Committee Minutes, April 3, 1975, 75-153-154.

53. On October 5, 1989, the General Conference Committee voted to refer to the 1990 General Conference Session a recommendation that: (1) women not be ordained, but that (2) commissioned women pastors "may perform essentially the ministerial functions of an ordained minister." But on October 9, the same committee voted to split that action, sending the recommendation that women not be ordained to 1990 General Conference Session, but immediately authorizing commissioned women pastors to "perform essentially the ministerial functions of an ordained minister." Source: General Conference Committee Minutes, October 5, 1989, 89-384-389, and October 9, 1989, 89-429-431 (see http://www.adventistarchives.org/gc-executive-committee-extracts-on-ordination.pdf).

Online Resources for Further Study

**Additional resources are available online at:
nadordination.com/read-more/**

2012 Seventh-day Adventist Women Clergy Conference, featuring speakers Ivan L. Williams, Esther Knott, Hyveth Williams, Ron du Preez, Dwight Nelson, Darius Jankiewicz, Stan Hickerson, and Tara VinCross. Online at http://www.nadministerial.org/article/250/for-nad-pastors/pastor-life/women-clergy/relive-the-2012-women-clergy-conference.

Benton, Josephine, *Called by God* (Blackberry Hill Publishing, 1990). Online at http://www.sdanet.org/atissue/books/called/index.htm.

Crocombe, Jeff, "Forgotten Heralds: Millerite Women Who Preached," Sept. 21, 2006. Online at http://h0bbes.wordpress.com/2006/09/21/forgotten-heralds-millerite-women-who-preached/

Crocombe, Jeff, "More Forgotten Heralds: Early Adventist Women Ministers," Oct. 1, 2006. Online at http://h0bbes.wordpress.com/2006/10/01/more-forgotten-heralds-early-adventist-women-ministers/

Crocombe, Jeff, "Irene Morgan," Nov. 6, 2006. Online at http://h0bbes.wordpress.com/2006/11/06/irene-morgan/

Fortin, Denis, "What Did Early Adventist Pioneers Think About Women in Ministry?" April 8, 2010. Online at http://www.memorymeaningfaith.org/blog/2010/04/adventist-pioneers-women-ministry.html

Jankiewicz, Darius, "The History of Ordination" (presentation at Sligo Seventh-day Adventist Church on July 28, 2012). Online at http://www.youtube.com/watch?v=ScKb3teILmI

"Methods of Bible Study: Presuppositions, Principles, and Methods" (Silver Spring, MD: General Conference of Seventh-day Adventists, 1986). Online at http://www.adventist.org/information/official-statements/documents/article/go/0/methods-of-bible-study/12/.

Questions and Answers About Women's Ordination

Nelson, Dwight, "A Mighty Throng of Women" (sermon at Pioneer Memorial Church on Oct. 6, 2012). Online at http://media.pmchurch.org/media/2012-10-06.mp4.

Nelson, Dwight, "Of Perfume and Tears and Grumpy Old Men," Part 2 in a series on The Last Days (sermon at Pioneer Memorial Church on Jan. 21, 2012). Online at http://vimeo.com/35596016 or http://media.pmchurch.org/media/2012-01-21.mp4.

North American Division Ministerial Department, "Roundtable Video" (Chestnut Hill Seventh-day Adventist Church members discuss their reactions to Tara VinCross being named senior pastor). Online at https://vimeo.com/59571048.

"North American Division Theology of Ordination Study Committee Report," November 2013. Online at http://nadordination.com.

Roberts, Randy, "Ordination Without Regard to Gender" (presentation at Pacific Union Conference special constituency session on August 19, 2012). Online at http://www.youtube.com/watch?v=UJPYohyzuuM&list=PL8E53FBD3B7907E0B&index=4

Roberts, Randy, "The Sixth Bad Idea: A Second-Class Ministry" Part 6 in a series on Seven Ideas That Ruined the Church . . . and Two Others That Didn't Help Any (sermon at Loma Linda University Church on March 10, 2012). Online at http://vimeo.com/38388120.

Rodríguez, Ángel Manuel, "Evaluation of the Arguments Used by Those Opposing the Ordination of Women to the Ministry" (paper presented at the Theology of Ordination Study Committee, Jan. 21-25, 2014). Online at http://nadordination.com/read-more/.

Valentine, Kendra Haloviak, "Junia: Inside Out," Part 3 in a series on God of the Outcast: Stories of Faith at the Margins (sermon at Azure Hills Seventh-day Adventist Church on July 28, 2012). Online at http://vimeo.com/46930336.

Valentine, Kendra Haloviak, and Bert Haloviak, "Adventist Women in Ministry—Progress or Regress?" (sermon at Azure Hills Seventh-day Adventist Church on March 22, 2014). Online at http://vimeo.com/89953603.

"Women Clergy Tell Their Stories" (collection of 81 audio recordings from women pastors). Online at http://www.nadministerial.org/article/237/for-nad-pastors/pastor-life/women-clergy/women-clergy-tell-their-stories.

Wolverton, Casey, "Is Ordination of Women a Theological or Cultural Issue?" (interview with Rebekah Liu posted Oct. 10, 2013). Online at http://www.youtube.com/watch?v=pGNJAP6zato.